PERSISTENT PREJUDICE
PERSPECTIVES ON
ANTI-SEMITISM

Edited by

Herbert Hirsch
and
Jack D. Spiro

George Mason University Press
Fairfax, Virginia

Copyright © 1988 by
George Mason University Press

4400 University Drive
Fairfax, VA 22030

Printed in the United States of America

Distributed by arrangement with
University Publishing Associates, Inc.

4720 Boston Way
Lanham, MD 20706

Library of Congress Cataloging-in-Publication Data

Persistent prejudice : perspectives on anti-Semitism / edited by
Herbert Hirsch and Jack D. Spiro.
p. cm.
Includes index.
1. Antisemitism. 2. Christianity and antisemitism.
3. Antisemitism—United States. I. Hirsch, Herbert, 1941–
II. Spiro, Jack D.
DS145.P416   1988
305.8'924'073—dc 19   87–32435 CIP
ISBN 0–913969–09–5 (alk. paper)

All George Mason University Press books are produced on acid-free
paper which exceeds the minimum standards set by the National
Historical Publications and Records Commission.

To our wives and children, we give our thanks and dedicate this volume with our profound wish that they might never experience the phenomena discussed here.

Contents

ACKNOWLEDGMENTS   viii

I. INTRODUCTION   1

II. RELIGIOUS AND IDEOLOGICAL EXPRESSIONS OF
ANTI-SEMITISM   5

   1. Anti-Semitism and Christianity: Theories and Revisions
of Theories

     Eugene J. Fisher   11

   2. Luther and the Roots of the Holocaust

     Richard L. Rubenstein   31

   3. Why People Kill: Conditions for Participation in
Mass Murder

     Herbert Hirsch   43

III. CULTURAL MANIFESTATIONS OF ANTI-SEMITISM   59

   4. A Historical Survey of Anti-Semitism in America
Prior to World War II

     Michael N. Dobkowski   63

   5. More Devils Than Hell Can Hold: Anti-Semitism in
American Literature

     Carole Kessner   83

   6. Shakespeare's Shylock and Ours

     Nicholas A. Sharp   99

IV. HOPEFUL CONCLUSIONS   107

   7. "That Marvellous Movement": Early Black Views of
Zionism

     Robert Weisbord and Richard Kazarian, Jr.   109

   8. Judaism and Christianity: Sources of Convergence

     Jack D. Spiro   133

INDEX   153

AUTHORS   158

Acknowledgments

We have many people to thank. If we forget anyone, we hope in the spirit of the book they will be tolerant and forgive us. First, we thank the Virginia Foundation for the Humanities and Public Policy, which provided a grant for partial funding of the original conference. The conference was also funded by a supplemental grant from the Judaic Culture Committee of Virginia Commonwealth University, which generously supplied us with advice as well as funds. The chair of that committee, Dr. Thomas O. Hall, was supportive of this effort throughout, as was Dr. Elske P. Smith, Dean of the College of Humanities and Sciences. In addition, we thank the Board of Managers and Harold Straus of Temple Beth Ahabah who donated their fine facility in which to hold the conference.

I

Introduction

Anti–Semitism has been one of the most persistent and deadly forms of prejudice of all time. As J. Milton Yinger noted in his important analysis:

Through the course of centuries it has illustrated all of the intricately related forces at work. It has ranged all the way from "polite" social exclusion to vicious pogroms. Insecure persons have found in the Jews a convenient scapegoat—available in almost every land, relatively powerless, distinguishable by religion and in some instances culture, and approved by tradition as a target for hostility. In almost every major economic or political conflict in the last several centuries one of the opposing forces, or both, has employed anti–Semitism as a weapon. Millions of people who have never known a Jew are equipped with a ready–made picture of his supposed physical appearance and personal characteristics.[1]

While many of the elements involved in anti–Semitism vary from case to case, others have remained relatively constant and underscore the strong probability that anti–Semitism, like other forms of prejudice, has deep historical and cultural roots. This book examines selected aspects of anti–Semitism, emphasizing its religious and ideological roots and cultural manifestations.

Most of the papers included here were first delivered at a conference on "Anti–Semitism in the United States" in Richmond, Virginia, in October of 1983. When we first proposed the conference, we were asked on several occasions, "Why talk about anti–Semitism? After all, the Holocaust is over, and it's no longer important. Do you really want to do this, when by doing so, you may stimulate anti–Semitic acts?"

We responded that we did want to bring anti–Semitism, in all its manifestations, to public awareness so that we are not trapped into complacently thinking that prejudice and discrimination vanish simply because they are expressed in less overt forms. We also recalled some overt expressions that indicate the continuing relevance of anti–Semitism:

- commentators in Europe and the United States who attempt to prove that the Holocaust did not occur or was the "fault" of the Jews;

- synagogues bombed and desecrated in widely separated communities;

- remarks of Christian clergy and Muslim leaders, even if later reinterpreted, that are clearly anti–Semitic;

- comments, such as one made by a student at the university where we teach, who wrote on his evaluation of a class taught by a Jewish professor, "I believe his Jewish culture blocks his viewpoints of the American way."

These few examples indicate that we are not dealing with an irrelevant or obsolete phenomenon, but a continuing expression of anti–Semitic feeling ranging from the subtle to the overt. As such, it represents the spectrum of prejudice and racism of which anti–Semitic ideologies and attitudes are a part. In an attempt to enrich understanding of the religious and ideological dynamics of anti–Semitism, we have put together this anthology.

To understand anti–Semitism, it is necessary to outline in brief its development from its ancient roots to its transformation by the Holocaust and the American experience. Historically, imagination was not lacking regarding the crimes attributed to Jews or in the policies framed to deal with these imagined crimes. Jews have been accused of, among other deeds, killing God or the son of God; being allied with the powers of evil; being hostile and unfriendly toward other religions; being homeless wanderers, the silent stranger; being unclean; being subversive of established religion or state; being carriers of new ideas; being usurers; being revolutionary; being communists; being capitalists; desecrating the host; poisoning wells; killing Christian children to use their blood in rituals; attempting to take over the world. Societies deal with these supposed "crimes" by subjecting Jews to measures including forced conversion, expulsion, pogroms, extermination, wearing badges of identification, isolation in ghettos, anti–Jewish laws, boycotts of Jewish enterprise, and assorted others, all determined by the fervent imagination of the anti–Semite.

Anti–Semitism has roots in antiquity, particularly in the countries of the Roman Empire. Jews were accused early on of being unfriendly "toward all Gentiles" and hostile to "every other religion."[2] Jews were viewed as nonconformists who, in their adherence to their religion, were seen as threatening and hostile toward other religions. Jews were the only people during this period, 175 to 164 B.C.E., "to deny the gods of their neighbors; to refrain from partaking of the sacrifices offered to their gods...[and to refuse] to send gifts to neighbors' temples;...[to be] hostile to intermarriage."[3] In short, "the belief gradually began to take hold in the pagan world that the Jews had no respect for whatever was held in esteem by the rest of humanity."[4] Despite this, the Jews of the pagan world were relatively free to work and live, and "no discrimination was made between them and the other citizens of the empire."[5] Rights were granted or denied primarily according to the class to which a person belonged.

As the era of Christianity approached, anti–Semitic views were elaborated further. Jews were increasingly portrayed as not only uncooperative, but also as unclean. Thus, "many Greek authors of the first century C.E. portrayed the Jewish people as the descendants of a mob of lepers, a contaminated rabble, whom the Egyptians had cast out to purge themselves of their defilement and who had continued to pursue in Judea, their adopted home, the pattern that accorded with their degenerate and outcast state."[6] While these overtly anti–Semitic characterizations grew in the pagan world, they could not match the ferocious and planned malevolent anti–Semitism that shifted from cultural and individual expression to active pursuit by the state.

Over time, three policies have been applied against the Jews: conversion, expulsion, and annihilation. Prior to the establishment of Christianity as the dominant religion, the Jews lived dispersed but relatively peacefully. When Christianity became the official religion, the state began to carry out church policy based on the anti–Semitic mythology referred to above. Jews were now defined as being outside the "Christian universe of obligation" and outside the state universe of obligation.[8] In effect, this left Jews unprotected, since they were not subjected to the laws designed to protect "ordinary" citizens. Consequently, "legal" victimization of the Jews became justified.

As Hilberg points out:

> For the next twelve centuries the Catholic Church prescribed the measures that were to be taken with respect to the Jews. Unlike the pre–Christian Romans, who claimed no monopoly on religion and faith, the Christian Church insisted upon acceptance of Christian doctrine....The Christian religion was not one of many religions like other religions. It was the true religion, the only religion.[9]

In such an atmosphere, from the eleventh to the thirteenth centuries, Jews were slain by roaming crusaders who sought to gain spiritual credit by murdering infidels. The First Crusade was a crucial event. Jewish areas of German and French towns were attacked. During the summer of 1096, massacres occurred. Even as European economic life began to revive in the twelfth century, Jews, already stigmatized as infidels and perpetrators of deicide, were regarded by most as direct antagonists to Christians and thus symbols of the hostile stranger in their midst.

At this point in history, many anti–Semitic myths were already in place, while others were still evolving. The notion of the Jew as both heretic and usurer was now being refined. In fact, according to contemporary idiom, the verb *to Judaize* meant to be a heretic and to lend money on interest.[10]

From the thirteenth to the sixteenth centuries, a second anti–Semitic policy was pursued. The Jews of England, France, Germany, Spain, Bohemia, and Italy were presented with ultimatums—they must convert or be expelled. Expulsion and exclusion, along with periodic pogroms, were established as state policy until 1942. Indeed, 1942 marks a turning point in anti–Jewish history, because the state, then in the form of Nazi Germany, began to pursue an articulated and planned policy of extermination.

To be sure, Jews were killed before 1942. From the Middle Ages on, they were lynched or killed after accusations of crimes such as poisoning wells believed to be the cause of bubonic plague, killing Christian children to extract their blood for ritual purposes, and desecrating the host used in Communion. Massacres were organized. Pogroms—episodic massacres sometimes staged to appear spontaneous—were common, especially during the period of the decline of the Russian Czars, beginning in the late nineteenth century. All anti–Jewish policies and ideas culminated in 1942 with the "final solution," which the Nazis justified by appealing to ideologies as diverse as Christian and German mythology. It is appropriate, therefore, to begin this volume with three essays that examine the ideological roots and consequences of anti–Semitism.

Notes

1. J. Milton Yinger, Jr., *Anti–Semitism: A Case Study in Prejudice and Discrimination* (New York: Freedom Books, 1964), p. 5, excerpted from George E. Simpson and J. Milton Yinger, Jr., *Racial and Cultural Minorities: An Analysis of Prejudice and Discrimination* (New York: Harper and Row, 1972).

2. Yizhak Heinemann et al., *Anti–Semitism,* Israel Pocket Library (Jerusalem: Keter, 1974), s.v. "Anti–Semitism." This collection, composed of material originally published in the *Encyclopaedia Judaica,* contains the single best summary of anti–Semitism. Unless otherwise noted, most of this introduction is derived from this source.

3. Ibid., p.3.

4. Ibid., p.5.

5. Ibid., p.6.

6. Ibid., p.8.

7. Raul Hilberg, *The Destruction of the European Jews* (New York: Harper and Row, 1961), pp. 1–17.

8. The most informative discussion of the "universe of obligation" is in Helen Fein, *Accounting for Genocide* (New York: The Free Press, 1979), pp. 8–9.

9. Hilberg, *Destruction,* p.1.

10. Heinemann et al., *Anti–Semitism,* p. 17.

II

Religious and Ideological Expressions of Anti-Semitism

Chapter 1 examines the ideological basis of anti-Semitism. In "Anti-Semitism and Christianity: Theories and Revisions of Theories," Fisher presents the major issues relating to the forces of anti-Semitism that stem from Christian sources. He treats the relationship between Jew and Christian chronologically, beginning with arguments for and against the thesis that anti-Semitism stems from the New Testament. He reviews the positions of such eminent scholars as Gregory Baum, Samuel Sandmel, and Rosemary Reuther. The latter argues forcefully that "the foundations of anti-Judaism were laid in the New Testament." As Fisher points out, Reuther's argument implies "that the link between Christianity and anti-Semitism was inevitable and perhaps indissoluble."

Fisher then considers the patristic period. Generally, it appears that the anti-Judaism we have come to associate with Christianity was not evident in this period. Only when we reach medieval Christianity do we percieve a "new state in anti-Semitism." Fisher sees the origins of Christian anti-Semitism in the writings and activities of the Dominicans and Franciscans, whose "vision of a society unified by one faith left less and less room for dissidents." The thirteenth century, according to Fisher and other scholars, was the turning point in Jewish-Christian relations—for the worse.

Thanks to Arthur Hertzberg's revisionist study of the Enlightenment, Fisher observes that in the eighteenth and nineteenth centuries, anti-Semitism appeared "with frightening ease to infect even the egalitarian reformers who brought about the emancipation of Jews from the ghettos." By the twentieth century, he notes, "Europe, religiously and ideologically divided, seemed to have just one point of unity: fear of Jews....Fear, of course, turns easily to hatred to mask itself...." Finally, Fisher can proclaim, "Nazism thus had a fertile field."

Chapter 2 turns to one set of ideological justifications for the "final solution." In "Luther and the Roots of the Holocaust," Rubenstein traces the enormous influence of Martin Luther's thought and delineates its relationship to a particularly virulent display of anti-Semitic violence. This analysis is central to any understanding of

5

anti–Semitism because it provides a basic example of the ideological foundation upon which anti–Semitic beliefs and violence may rest.

In this provocative essay, Rubenstein points out that "Luther did as much to discover the new world of the spirit as Columbus did to discover the territorial New World." Luther, Rubenstein argues, "can be seen as one of [the]... primary creators" of our world, putting as he did "the whole weight" of "religious commitment on faith" in Scripture. This meant that any challenge to his system of beliefs had to be discredited, and it was "the unfortunate destiny of the Jews to challenge, simply by fidelity to their own tradition, what was absolutely fundamental to Luther, his reading of Scripture."

Luther's emphasis on the centrality of faith is exemplified by his trenchant comment "that he would rather be a sow than be a man without Christ, because a sow does not have the fear and anxiety to which natural man is condemmed after the Fall." Man can be reconciled to God, according to Luther, only by acts of God, not man, and the "good news" is "found solely in Scripture." Commenting on the central importance of Luther's revisionism, Rubenstein points out, "Luther has abandoned the medieval hope that man can rise from nature to supernature through this–worldly means.... Everything now depends upon the truth of Scripture's account of God's promises."

In 1543, responding to his perception of Jewish challenges to his interpretation of Scripture, Luther wrote his most "violently anti–Jewish work," *On the Jews and Their Lies*. This tract, later used as a model for the maniacal fulminations in Hitler's anti–Semitic arsenal, is the centerpiece of Luther's anti–Semitism. Here even the most seasoned analyst can find shocking examples. For Luther there is no ambiguity; for Luther, Rubenstein explains, the "Jews are of the Devil." Luther demanded that they be expelled from Germany and advocated overt violence against the Jews and their institutions, at one point stating, "We are at fault in not slaying them." Violence against the Jews, moreover, was rationalized intrinsically.

"Jewish misfortune," to use Rubenstein's term, provides for Luther and other "Christian thinkers, both ancient and modern," the best refutation of "Jewish reading of Scripture." Anti–Semitic beliefs and acts are interpreted as "decisive proof of God's rejection of the Jews." If the Jews' reading of Scripture were congruent with God's, they would not have been punished so severely. In short, these blatantly anti–Semitic sentiments constitute what Rubenstein terms a "religiously legitimized incitement to homicidal violence." He points out that leading German theologians in the 1930s used *On the Jews and Their Lies* to justify policies pursued by the Nazis. In fact, as Rubenstein tells us, "Bishop Otto Dibelius, who was to serve as president of the World Council of Churches in 1965, saw the National Socialist policies towards the Jews as fulfillment of Luther's program." The end result of Luther's energetic denunciation of the Jews served to define them as outside the "universe of moral obligation" and consequently subject to repression and destruction without protection by state or religion. Rubenstein states in an important passage: ...we had better be warned by Luther's example. In times of minimal social stress, exclusive religions can live in relative peace with one another, especially when relations among them are clearly defined. Unfortunately, we have seen all too many examples of periods of heightened social stress during which religious and communal strife intensify to the point of large–scale violence. The Reformation was such a time. So too was World War II....Luther's demonization of the Jews and Judaism in the fifteenth century, which in its turn reiterated the view of the Jews found in the Gospels, gave sacred sanction in the twentieth century to a view of the Jews as enemies wholly outside any conceivable German universe of obligation.

As Rubenstein sums up, while Luther "did not create the gas chambers, he did contribute significantly to their indispensable precondition, the denial of the Jews' humanity and their transformation into Satan's spawn." Thus, the full effect of Luther's denunciations were not manifested until World War II. Rubenstein illustrates perceptively how religious ideology can serve as justification for mass murder—even that occurring hundreds of years later.

The third essay in this collection takes this analysis another step and illustrates how these and other factors might be translated into the act of murder. In "Why People Kill: Conditions for Participation in Mass Murder," Hirsch examines the cultural, psychological, and political conditions that conceivably might motivate people to participate in acts of mass murder. Using the Holocaust as an example, Hirsch starts with the premise that "for mass murder to proceed, mechanisms must be developed to short–circuit traditional concepts of individual morality. Psychologically, people must not be allowed to feel guilty when they destroy others." The basic question becomes, what are "the conditions that allow mass murder to take place without any guilt manifested at all?"

The cultural conditions for mass murder are the most general. According to Hirsch, they "usually are tied to the myths and ideologies stressed in a culture or nation state." Using the example of the Nazis, Hirsch points out how they "invoked the ideas of blood and soil in their myth." Appealing to pre–Christian times to rationalize the "final solution," Jews were dehumanized in a manner congruent with the portrait drawn by Luther in *On the Jews and Their Lies.* "Following Luther and other philosophers of Aryan superiority, Hitler believed in the worldwide Jewish conspiracy and that Jews were vermin and lice." The dehumanizing stereotypes are keys to the creation of what Hirsch calls a "target population" for which extermination becomes a justifiable policy. The dehumanizing images over time may become part of a culture, creating a relationship between dehumanizing symbols and the cultural conditions and ultimately the psychological conditions.

The psychological conditions for mass murder, according to Hirsch, "focus directly on the possibility that, given the right circumstances, any individual might be placed in a position in which his or her morality, or sense of right and wrong, is compromised." The basic psychological conditions depend on unquestioning obedience to authority. Following the pioneering work of Stanley Milgram, Hirsch proposes that when individuals learn that obedience takes precedence over all other considerations, people come to "define themselves as instruments for carrying out the wishes of others. The classic example...is Adolf Eichmann"; the classic explanation is Hannah Arendt's idea of the "banality of evil."

According to this notion, as Hirsch reiterates, acts of ultimate evil are "not necessarily committed by noticeably psychopathic deranged monsters" but instead "by very ordinary people" following orders without question. And the author points out that these controversial hypotheses "force us to focus on our own vulnerability and to question the circumstances of obedience." Finally, the psychology of mass murder is closely linked to politics.

This third set of conditions, argues Hirsch, is tied to culture as well as psychology. Political socialization provides the transition as the process through which people learn about the culture into which they are born. Through a series of agents, every person learns, among other things, the existing definitions of politics and morality. If a nation or culture contains threads of an ethos that emphasizes "rigidity and obedience," and these are transmitted to individuals and ultimately internalized by them, "then these cultural imperatives stressing obedience become preconditions for participation in mass murder." According to Hirsch, additional aspects of the political conditions involve, first, the avoidance of responsibility, and, second, the justification and encouragement by political leaders. "Basically, the cultural myths are reinforced and transmitted through political socialization. Mass murder is committed in the name of some higher good....Acts of guilt–free massacre are justified and responsibility is diffused."

Hirsch summarizes:

The cultural conditions, which involve the development of cultural and racial myths and racial stereotypes, provide the environment for the victimization of a target population....The psychological conditions [require] an obedience to authority by individuals, the people, who will pull the triggers and carry out the orders. The political conditions combine the giving of orders and justification for the acts of destruction.

This analysis underscores, as Hirsch concludes, the need to "understand the past and incorporate as an integral part of our learning experience" material that explains how and why such horrific events as the Holocaust occurred. Consequently, it is important to examine specific cultures as a means to uncover clues to possible expressions of anti-Semitism. The next section of this collection looks into "Cultural Manifestations of Anti-Semitism."

Chapter 1

Anti-Semitism and Christianity: Theories and Revisions of Theories

Eugene J. Fisher

The Holocaust took place in a part of the world that was long deemed Christian. It was perpetuated to an appalling extent by people who saw themselves as "good" Christians even while organizing the meticulous details of coldly calculated genocide. This basic fact has raised, in the wake of the event, fundamental questions concerning the theology and practice of the Christianity in which the perpetrators had been reared. How, it has been rightly asked, could generations of hearing the gospel message of love and forgiveness, in the twentieth century, issue in a generation in which so many of the catechized were willing either to participate in or cast a blind eye upon the suffering of the very people of Jesus from whom their ancestors had learned of the God of love and compassion?

Half a century after the first racial laws were promulgated in Germany, the question is still being asked. Pope John Paul II, a Pole who himself saw the scourge of Nazi brutality sear his homeland, has called poignantly for a thorough revision of Christian teaching in regard to the Jews and Judaism:

> It is necessary to get to the point where such teaching at the various levels of religious instruction and catechesis with children and adolescents will not only present the Jews and Judaism in an honest and objective manner, but will also do so without any prejudice or offense to anyone and, even more, with a lively awareness of...our common spiritual heritage [which is] above all important at the level of our faith....Certainly, since a new bough appeared from the common root 2,000 years ago, we know that relations between our two communities have been marked by resentments and a lack of understanding. If there have been misunderstandings, errors and even insults since the day of separation, it is now a question of overcoming them with understanding, peace and mutual esteem. The terrible persecutions suffered by the Jews in various periods of history have finally opened many eyes and disturbed many hearts.[1]

11

This recent challenge to Christian teaching, as the Pope acknowledges, does not come in isolation, but stands upon a vast and growing body of scholarship and Christian–Jewish dialogue that seeks to probe the ambiguities of a complex past in order to shape an authentic path for a future relationship.[2] Even while Nazi Germany was gearing up the machinery of death, scholars such as Karl Barth and Jacques Maritain were initiating the review of fundamental Christian thought on Judaism.[3]

Following the liberation of the camps, the great French Jewish historian Jules Isaac began the first systematic approach to the relationship between Christian teaching and anti–Semitism.[4] The path of Western anti–Semitism, Isaac argued, could be traced back to certain Christian theses, such as supercessionism and the deicide charge, which by the time of the Church fathers in the fourth and fifth centuries had congealed into a Christian "teaching of contempt" toward Jews that was to prevail for centuries. Isaac's schema saw Christian thought as, if not inventing (one can point out many examples of pagan anti–Semitism), then at least embellishing Western anti–Judaism with particular features of the Christian theology of contempt. This, in turn, set the stage for the full–blown anti–Semitism of the nineteenth and twentieth centuries that resulted in the Nazi *endlosung* of "the Jewish problem."

Since Isaac's time, a growing literature has scrutinized this hypothesis both historically and theologically. It would take a substantial volume simply to undertake a thorough review of this literature. This paper, instead, will articulate chronologically a few of the major issues involved, indicate where consensus exists among the scholars and where it does not. No attempt has been made to be exhaustive or inclusive on any of these issues. The thinkers discussed are representative and not necessarily the best on any particular point.

The New Testament and Anti–Semitism

Gregory Baum, in the introduction to his 1961 study, *The Jews and the Gospel*, acknowledged that "it is in partial criticism of this great book (*Jesus and Israel*) that this book is written."[5] Baum did not seek to refute Isaac's central thesis that the Christian teaching of contempt laid the groundwork for modern anti–Semitism with its overwhelmingly negative portrait of Jews. Baum argues, rather, that a clear line should be drawn when it comes to the New Testament:

> In the New Testament itself, according to Jules Isaac, we find the beginning of a movement which aims at regarding the Jews as an outcast people and which ends, after a transposition of keys and the amalgamation with other currents of thought, in the cold and calculated hatred of modern anti–Semitism....This supposition is one a Christian must reject, and reject vehemently. It is unthinkable for anyone who ac-

cepts the gospel as the ultimate revelation of divine love that part of the New Testament was designed to encourage contempt of any people and contribute, in a direct way, to the growth of misunderstanding and hatred in the world.[6]

Baum proceeds to engage in a meticulous account of the New Testament, book by book, concluding with a treatment of St. Paul, especially in Romans 9 through 11. His study shows, reasonably successfully, that acceptance of the New Testament message as a whole, properly understood, does not lead to anti–Semitism. A problem surfaces, however, with what in retrospect can be seen as a confusion over the definition of the precise question at hand. Baum's revised 1966 edition shows that he perceived the issue at the time as an all or nothing choice: his title asks, *Is the New Testament Anti–Semitic?*

Isaac's work, however, had not accused the New Testament of anti–Semitism. Rather, he had argued that in the process of its development during the first century after the death of Jesus, various polemical strands had become embedded in the New Testament. These, when exploited by later Christians, became all too susceptible to being used as justifications for anti–Semitic attacks. Isaac pointed out, for example, that the later gospels tended to whitewash the role of the Roman governor, Pilate, in the events of the crucifixion, giving increasing prominence to the Jewish role and paving the way for the devastating deicide charge at the center of the theological architecture of the teaching of contempt.[7]

Samuel Sandmel subtly modified the title of his 1978 parallel study of Baum, *Anti–Semitism in the New Testament?*, to illustrate the importance of how the question is framed. While Baum's question (*Is the New Testament Anti–Semitic?*) can lead to a challenge of the essential integrity and validity of the divine inspiration of the apostolic writings, the latter question raises the hermeneutical challenge to Christians of how to cope with varying New Testament attitudes toward Jews, some of which are positive and some of which are negative. The Christian today need not accept or reject the New Testament as such, but should understand its message shorn of historically conditioned prejudice. On this level, I believe, Isaac asks Christians to rethink the implications of their faith. Sandmel, along this line, was able to conclude his trenchant portrait of the anti–Semitic polemical material in the gospels on a positive note: "I firmly believe on the basis of my experience with Christians...that once full recognition [of the problem] takes place and the will exists, the solution will be found. Not all at once, and not in a single step, but surely it will come."[8]

Rosemary Reuther's *Faith and Fratricide* dramatically reposed the question from a Christian point of view and, ironically, obscured the question. Her study appears to establish that the New Testament polemics against the Jews are related to the development of "high"

Christology. As a result, anti-Semitism might fairly be called "the left hand of Christology." For Reuther, Christology itself becomes the "key issue."

We have seen that the anti-Judaic myth is neither a superficial nor a secondary element in Christian thought. The foundations of anti-Judaism were laid in the New Testament. They were developed in the classical age of Christian theology in a way that laid the basis for attitudes and practices that continually produced terrible results.[9]

Such a statement, seemingly drawing a straight line from the Gospel of John to the crematoriums of Auschwitz, goes significantly beyond Isaac's carefully worded theses, arguing that the link between Christianity and anti-Semitism was inevitable and perhaps indissoluble. Along with Gregory Baum's dramatic rejection in his introduction to Reuther's book of his earlier defensive posture toward the Scriptures,[10] Reuther poses an unresolvable dilemma for the Christian. Must one repudiate Christianity in order to repudiate anti-Semitism?

As subsequent study has shown, this was a false dilemma. Samuel Sandmel neatly responded to it:

Is anti-Semitism indeed beyond total eradication from Christian minds and hearts? Surely the New Testament...can be used to so argue, as Rosemary Reuther seems to feel. But Reuther in a sense personifies the refutation of herself. That she could think and write as she did surely points the way. What seems to be needed is precisely that frankness which characterizes both Reuther and her thoughtful critics.[11]

An excellent, representative sample of this thoughtful criticism of the Reutherian thesis can be found in the twelve essays collected by Alan T. Davies in *Anti-Semitism and the Foundations of Christianity*. These essays acknowledge that religious polemic directed at Judaism is used as a literary device in various strata of the development of the New Testament as we have it today. Still, other theological options more positive toward Jews are embodied also in the apostolic witness. Davies comments that the essays he edited

examine the emergence of the Christian faith in the polemical and tumultuous atmosphere of the ancient world. The interplay of Christian, Jewish and pagan attitudes is brought into relief in order to shed light on a complex process. If a common motif in these essays can be described, it is the conviction that Christians need not choose between an ideological defense of their scriptures that wards off damaging criticism and the sad conclusion that the New Testament is so wholly contaminated by anti-Jewish prejudice as to lose all moral authority. Instead, through careful study, Christians can isolate what genuine forms of anti-Judaism really color the major writings and, by examining their historic genesis, neutralize their potential for harm.[12]

The Patristic Period

Again, a tremendous effort has gone into researching and refining the issues of the patristic period. Some consensus appears to be emerging. First, I note the modern revival of the charge issued by some of the most ancient Christian writers,[13] apparently expanding on hints in the Gospel of John,[14] of an expulsion of Christians from the Synagogue late in the first century by means of inclusion of the so-called curse against the *minim* (heretics) in the *Shemoneh Esreh*, the daily prayer.

The problem with this theory, which has gained some popularity in Christian circles, is that no rabbinic evidence suggests that *minim* was only understood to include Christians (*nosrim*-Nazarites) many centuries later, when *nosrim* was, in the wake of negative perspectives of Jews by Christians, added to some versions of the prayer.[15] Likewise, the continuing complaints of Christian bishops well into the ninth century that their flocks were spending too much time in the synagogues and with the rabbis would militate against any notion of a universal expulsion of Christians from the synagogues. (Certainly, it could not have been a very effective one.) It would seem that this theory, as was the case with Baum's earlier work, essentially is motivated by apology.

A larger and more central question in the scholarship concerning this period is the relative influence of pagan anti-Jewishness on the Christian variety. On the one hand, the notion put forward by some Christian apologists holds that since anti-Jewish writings abound among the classical pagan authors of antiquity, Christianity cannot be said to have invented anti-Judaism but merely (albeit unfortunately) carried forward in history a virulent strain that originated in an earlier conflict between monotheism and polytheism.[16] In this vein, much could be made of statements by Jewish scholars that, as Salo Baron put it, "almost every note in the cacaphony of medieval and modern anti-Semitism was sounded by a chorus of ancient writers."[17] Similarly, Marcel Simon has said that "they tend, perhaps unconsciously, to make this purely literary (pagan) anti-Semitism something artificial and in this way acquit pagan opinion in order to cast upon the Church the whole responsibility."[18]

How the question is posed, then, is not without relevance when interpreting the literature. Lovsky has summarized neatly what Edward Flannery calls "the tendentiousness of historians in this period of anti-Semitism."[19]

When the bias of the historian [is Christian], the alibis of Egyptians (or Persians) are gladly featured, as if the sin of the pagan should attenuate that of the Christians; when it is anti–Christian, the protests against the existence of Egyptian anti–Semitism are so much greater in order to burden the Church with an animosity that would find its inspiration in the Christian faith. Indeed because of such reservations, impartial debate would seem impossible.[20]

Flannery, warning against such lack of objectivity on either side in his classic study, *The Anguish of the Jews*, attempts a balanced presentation in which the specific theological contribution of Christian anti–Judaic tradition to the history of anti–Semitism is not lost from sight.[21]

Rosemary Reuther characteristically carries further the approaches of Isaac and Simon by stressing the differences between pagan and Christian anti–Jewish writings to emphasize the essential independence of the latter from the former. She notes that the overall attitude toward Judaism in the ancient world was not essentially hostile and that, with the exception of specific conflicts, it was rather one of "mutual cooperation that would respect Jewish distinctiveness."[22]

Two recent works add substantially to an unapologetic treatment of the period. Robert L. Wilken's *John Chrysostum and the Jews* sets "the golden mouth" (whose anti–Jewish diatribes contributed much to the hardening of Christian attitudes toward Jews in the Middle Ages) in the context of an Antioch of relative pluralism and prosperity, where Jews, Christians, and pagans all represented vital, creative communities.[23] So vital was the Jewish community, in Wilken's view, that its rituals and practices held great attraction for pagan and Christian alike. Thus Chrysostum, in developing his *Homiliae adversars Judaeos*, would have felt himself to be presenting a defensive as opposed to an offensive argument, attempting to call back Christian "Judaizers" to the churches rather than aiming at a triumphant destruction of Judaism. Wilken, in his defense of Chrysostum, blames anti–Semitism on later generations of Christians who, having lost the knowledge of the specific devices of classical rhetoric that Chrysostum employed, took his writings with deadly and literal earnestness. Wilken then concludes:

> When I began to study John Chrysostum's writings on the Jews, I was inclined to judge what he said in light of the unhappy history of Jewish–Christian relations and the sad events in Jewish history in modern times....I am no longer ready to project these later attitudes onto the events of the fourth century....The medieval image of the Jews should not be imposed on antiquity.[24]

The apparent parallel between this revisionist defense of Chrysostum (and by extension of the church fathers who participated in the creation of the *adversus Judaeos* tradition) and Gregory Baum's initial defense of the New Testament on similar grounds is inescapable.

Yet Wilken's position actually may be closer in spirit to that of the consensus of modified Reutherian scholars represented in the Davies collection. Wilken does not hesitate to distance himself from John's theology, even while arguing that it differs essentially from the demonization of the Jews that took place in the High Middle Ages.[25]

John's homilies are part of a Christian interpretation of Judaism that must be subjected to theological criticism. Like many early Christian thinkers, John assumed that the rise of Christianity and the destruction of the city of Jerusalem, events that seemed co-terminous [though they took place more than a generation apart], meant that Judaism had lost its theological legitimacy....Such confidence about the theological meaning of the fall of Jerusalem, though self-evident to many Christians of John's day, is no longer possible....The Jewish people, and the practice of Judaism, have persisted, indeed prevailed....Indeed, whatever the religious meaning of the fall of Jerusalem, its significance today can only be measured by the equally important events of the survival of the Jewish people after the Holocaust and the establishment of the modern state of Israel.[26]

Similarly, Gregory Baum, in his contribution to the Davies volume, sees biblical messages of life as a hermeneutical principle by which to judge the New Testament's polemical strata:

Since, in the history of the West, the spiritual negation of Jewish existence has led to contempt, injustices and, however indirectly, physical extermination, the traditional teaching stood condemned by a superior principle, namely the redemption of human life, which constitutes the spirit and substance of the Bible....Because of this supreme biblical teaching, it is possible to correct certain positions of scripture and tradition when they serve the destruction of life and the enslavement of human beings.[27]

Along the same lines, New Testament scholar Raymond Brown argues that the Church ought to read the entire Passion during Holy Week,

but that, once having read it, then to preach forcefully that such hostility between Christian and Jew cannot be continued today and is against our fundamental understanding of Christianity. Sooner or later Christian believers must wrestle with the limitations imposed on the Scriptures by the circumstances in which they were written.[28]

In his *Origins of Anti-Semitism*, John G. Gager of Princeton sets out to test the "consensus and crisis" in modern scholarship, especially in response to Reuther. He points out, for example, that in some ways "the distance between Reuther and her critics is not great," since she too concedes that "the early Church did not think of the message of the crucified and risen messiah as putting them outside or against Judaism."[29] To the extent this was true, it cannot be said that the polemical strains of the New Testament represent anti–Judaism (much less modern anti–Semitism), for the authors would have seen themselves more as reformers in the prophetic mold. Again, the onus falls on later generations of gentile Christians who, reading the New Testament from outside Jewish tradition, transformed a limited internal Jewish debate into an absolute condemnation of Jews and Judaism.

Gager tends to mediate between this notion (which would let the New Testament off the hook) and the more thorough assessment of the New Testament as anti–Semitic that Reuther, despite her occasional caveats, appears to be driving at. In the Synoptics and John, Gager finds varying degrees of "gentilizing" anti–Judaism along with a modicum of the "prophetic," intra–Jewish variety.[30] The Epistle to the Hebrews is seen as "well on the way toward Marcion"[31] and the reduction of the debate between Christians and Jews into full–blown anti–Jewish diatribe.[32]

Following the lead of "Gaston's radical reappraisal" of St. Paul, which he feels "challenges Reuther on every major issue, including the linkage of Christology and anti–Judaism," Gager makes a major contribution to the contemporary effort to "reinvent" Paul, an effort that also owes much to the work of Standahl, Sloyan, Mussner, Koenig, and Sanders.[33] Paul's arguments, Gager unassailably notes following Gaster, were aimed at Christians (whether of Gentile or Jewish origin), not at Jews.[34] For Paul, the relationship between Torah and Christ "is such that neither invalidates the other. Torah remains the path of righteousness for Israel; Christ has become the promised way of righteousness for Gentiles."[35]

While the importance of Gager's final section on Paul momentarily has brought us back to our earlier subject, the bulk of the work does belong to the subject at hand.[36] Gager's point is to critique the notion admittedly shared by most scholars that the categories of "anti–Semite" or "anti–Judaism" do not portray adequately the complex reality of Jewish–Gentile relations in the ancient world in which Christianity developed. Thus, his revisionist thrust is similar to Wilken's, which provides significant evidence for the positive attraction of Judaism to pagans and Christians in the fourth century. Gager's scope, however, is a bit wider than Wilken's, delving back to the third century before the common era to marshal his evidence. His thesis is summarized in his introduction:

> Put simply, the real problem [of modern scholarship] lies...in the tendency to use terms like anti–Semitism and anti–Judaism in a global manner, as if they encompassed the full range of interactions between Jews and non–Jews in antiquity. However understood, anti–Semitism and anti–Judaism tell

only part of the story, and therein lies the basic issue. Only in a highly restricted sense can Western anti-Semitism be said to originate in pagan and Christian antiquity. The presumption of a universal anti-Semitism in antiquity, pagan or Christian, has been made possible only by suppressing, ignoring or misinterpreting the mass of non-conforming evidence.[37]

Gager amasses evidence to refute the Reutherian dictum that "antiquity, on the whole, disliked the Jews." This remark, Gager feels, "does a disservice to its intended apologetic and is untrue to the facts." Rather, following the work of Israeli scholars Menahem Stern and Shimon Applebaum, Gager argues that there existed among Greeks and Romans "a remarkable degree of sympathy for Judaism."[38]

Excursus: Anti-Semitism in Christian Scholarship

We have seen enough by now to note one of the major problems of the field: the relative degrees of academic objectivity among many of those engaged in it. John Gager comments on this in his review of the literature, along with the fact that so many scholars involved primarily have been motivated by theological concerns. Citing studies made of the historical treatment of Jews in Christian scholarly works over the last several decades, by such scholars as Moore, Klein, and Sanders,[39] Gager tells us:

> To read this [literature] is a disheartening experience. The works surveyed there are influential and representative. The optimistic judgment of several Jewish and Christian scholars to the effect that Christian scholarship on Judaism has finally been purged would seem to be somewhat premature;...much of Christian scholarship on ancient Judaism has been shaped by the legacy of early Christian anti-Judaism.[40]

Thus, while the majority of scholars discussed here can be said to be free of the "legacy of contempt," we must remember that these scholars write against a background of modern Christian scholarship in which that legacy is all too apparent, even in its standards, in the work of Schurer, Bultmann, Bousset, Strack-Billerbeck, Bornkamm, Kasemann, and Conzelmann.[41] Likewise, Protestant scholars such as George Foote Moore and E.P. Sanders have noted that Protestant (especially continental European) scholarship at times has obscured even further the understanding of Jewish-Christian relations in the early period by projecting aspects of Roman Catholic belief and practice deemed distasteful to the Jews, thus turning objective scholarship into what Gager calls "a covert polemic against Roman Catholicism."[42] Such intellectual shenanigans have further muddied the already troubled waters of modern scholarship on the history of Christian-Jewish relations (of which Christian anti-Semitism is a subset).

Before coming to any general conclusions, one must be especially careful about secondary sources.[43]

Medieval Christianity: A New State in Anti-Semitism

An important testimony to the essential validity of the more balanced views of the relations between Jews and Christians in the first millenium of their interaction comes from recent studies of developments in the High Middle Ages (loosely, the twelfth to the sixteenth centuries), the period that saw the Inquisition rise and flourish. One of the strongest challenges to Reuther's theory of direct causal linkage between New Testament theology and Nazi genocide came, in fact, from a Jewish scholar of the Inquisition, Yosef Hayim Yerushalmi, at an international symposium on the Holocaust held at New York's Cathedral Church of St. John the Divine in 1974.[44] Yerushalmi does not for a moment deny the tragic effects of Christian anti-Jewish polemic on Western history. Like Gager and Wilken, however, he wishes to remind us of the other "variables" that Reuther "has left out" of her telling of the story. The real question, Yerushalmi argues, is not why Christians were so often violent and hate-filled in their treatment of Jews. The question is, given the tremendous negative effect of the teaching of contempt, "why did they [the Christians] not destroy the Jews?"[45]

Reuther's approach, Yerushalmi notes, dwells exclusively on the theory of reprobation of the Jews. But one also finds a functioning theory of preservation. Whereas the temples and institutions of pagans and heretics were destroyed or confiscated by Christianity once it gained power as the state religion of the Roman Empire, Judaism did not suffer the same fate. Synagogues were protected by law and, contrary to Reuther's depiction of the Jew in Christendom "as a person without honor or civil rights," medieval Jewry enjoyed "an entire gamut of well-defined rights which, on the whole, made the socioeconomic status of the Jews superior to that of the Christian peasantry who often constituted the bulk of the population." Further, Yerushalmi feels, Reuther "discusses the Church in a curiously monolithic way."[46] Often popes and kings would rise to the protection of the Jewish community, as in the case of the infamous blood libel charges. And the periodically renewed papal legislation known as the *Constitutio Pro Judaeis*, ambiguous as it was in its attitude toward Jews,[47] at least offered a court of appeal for the protection of Jewish rights.

"From Rosemary Reuther," Yerushalmi concludes, "we gather that genocide against the Jews was an inexorable consequence of Christian theological teaching."[48] This is what he wishes to question, for "if it were genocide it should have come upon the Jews in the Middle Ages," when the Church had for all practical purposes total physical control over their fate. He continues:

There is no question but that Christian anti–Semitism through the ages helped create the climate and mentality in which genocide, once conceived, could be achieved with little or no opposition. But even if we grant that Christian teaching was a necessary cause leading to the Holocaust, it was surely not a sufficient one. The crucial problem in the shift from medieval to modern anti–Semitism is that while the Christian tradition of "reprobation" continued into the modern era, the Christian tradition of "preservation" fell by the wayside. To state only that modern anti–Semitism is a "transformed" medieval anti–Semitism is to skirt this central issue. Surely there must be more significance in the fact that the Holocaust took place in our secular century and *not* in the Middle Ages....State–inspired pogroms of the type that took place in Czarist Russia, state–instigated genocide of the Nazi type—these are entirely modern phenomena. The climactic anti–Jewish measure of which the medieval Christian state was capable was always expulsion and, on rare occasions, forced conversion. The Holocaust was the work of a thoroughly modern, non–pagan state.[49]

Just as Reuther insists on the discontinuity between the anti–Jewish polemics of the ancient pagan world and the pointedly theological polemics of the patristic period, so does Yerushalmi point out the discontinuity between the ambivalent attitudes of Christian theory regarding the Jews and the genocidal anti–Semitism developed under secular, even scientific, guise in the rise of nineteenth– and twentieth–century racial anti–Semitism. The Jews of Christendom could escape the difficulties imposed on them through conversion. Under Hitler, there was no escape, only death.

Lest the measured counsel of Professor Yerushalmi lead Christians to feel that the historical burden is entirely lifted, however, the recent work of Jeremy Cohen, *The Friars and the Jews*, reminds us of the darker side of the history of Christian theology. For some, it would seem, a classical ambivalence favored reprobation and its consequences alone. Among them, according to Cohen, were especially the mendicant orders, the Dominicans and the Franciscans, who from the twelfth to the sixteenth centuries developed a more dangerous anti–Judaic theology and who spread it so successfully that by the end of the sixteenth century, Jews had nearly disappeared from Western Europe.[50]

In line with Wilken and Gager, Cohen presumes an overall situation of tolerance and mutual interaction between Jews and Christians during the first twelve centuries of their coexistence. Despite their reprobate status, Jews held, in Christian theory, a positive role as well. As Augustine put it, the Jewish witness to the Hebrew Scriptures was divinely ordained: "We see and know that it is in order to bear this witness—which they [the Jews] involuntarily supply on our behalf by possessing and preserving these same books—that they themselves are scattered among all peoples, in whatever direction the Church of Christ expands."[51]

First the Dominicans and later the Franciscans, Cohen argues, developed a distinct new theology of the relationship between the Church and the Jewish people, one that reflected the needs of their inquisitorial and missionary efforts. Not coincidentally, it may be noted, during this period, Christian treatment of Jews took a decidedly ugly turn. Jews were massacred throughout Europe in the wake of the great plague of the fourteenth century (for which, of course, they were blamed). The blood libel charges became widespread. Passion plays stressing the deicide charge became common, as did expulsions. In this period, too, the ghettos were first enforced in Italy, and the Fourth Lateran Council significantly modified (in the negative direction) the old tolerance of canonical legislation, coming up with the idea of distinctive clothing (based on Muslim models) to mark off Jews.

The Dominicans, Cohen's research shows, began the theoretical shift by beginning the study of the Talmud, both as a prooftext to use against Jews in the disputations and as a source of heresy. The Jewish community was no longer seen merely as a remnant of biblical Israel to be converted before the end of time, a fossilized vestige useful as a handy proof of Christian triumph. Rather, rabbinic literature, for the first time, was itself taken note of and seen as a source of heresy—primarily for Jews and then for Christians. As the mendicant theology spread, even the popes acquiesced in the burning of the Talmud. The developing vision of a society unified by one faith left less and less room for dissidents, in principle and in practice, and expulsions became common, beginning in the thirteenth century and culminating, but not ending, with the trauma of the expulsion from Spain and Portugal at the end of the fifteenth century.

As Cohen describes it, the thirteenth century was a turning point in Christian history. The separation of Jews and Christians was enforced by walls both of stone and of theology. What Chrysostom may have sighed for became reality for the first time.

From the thirteenth century onward, anti–Jewish violence increased throughout Europe. Only from this period were Jews portrayed as real, active agents of Satan, charged with innumerable forms of hostility toward Christianity, Christendom, and individual Christians. Blood libels and charges of host desecration first appeared in medieval Europe in the thirteenth century. In this century, the representation of Jews in Christian art became noticeably more hostile and demeaning, with the first examples of the infamous *Judensau* (portrayals of Jews sucking at the teats of a sow) and the frequent juxtaposition of the Jews and the devil. No longer were Jews depicted like their Christian neighbors or as mere symbols in the drama of religious history; they had become pernicious enemies of Christians and the Church, and pictorially they often came to represent the archetypical heretics.[52] In short, new elements had been added to the anti–Semitic tradition, elements upon which even the nineteenth– and twentieth–century variety of the virus, irreligious and even antireligious as it was, would not scruple to draw. It may be said that this demonization of the Jews in popular Christian thought became so pervasive that not even the great leaders of the Reformation sought to reform it.

The Reformation: Anti–Judaism as a Point of Continuity From Medieval to Modern Society

In his *Roots of Anti–Semitism in the Age of Renaissance and Reformation*, Heiko Obermann, the great Luther scholar, demonstrates the links between the medieval and modern periods in the development of anti–Judaic theory and practice within Christianity.[53] Obermann's study began with an invitation to contribute a paper on "Luther and the Jews." But Obermann soon realized that Luther's anti–Jewish polemics, whether of the milder, conversionist variety found in the 1523 treatise, *That Jesus Christ was Born a Jew*, or the wholly vituperative 1543 tract, *On the Jews and Their Lies*, could not be properly understood outside the wider context of Luther's times.

Obermann thus analyzes concisely the attitudes towards Jews and Judaism of the major reformers, from Melancthon and Oslander to Justus Jonas and John Calvin, as well as their principal scholastic opponents and even the leading humanists of the late Renaissance (Reuchlin, Erasmus, and others). He finds that all of the great figures of the age, as diverse as they were on almost every other issue, stood united as anti–Jew. While the seeds of tolerance may have been sown in the often bloody internecine Christian rivalries of the period, they did not flower for some centuries. Even Reuchlin's interest in defending access to Hebrew texts turns out to have been motivated less by disinterested scholarship than by many of the same fears and phobias about "Jewish magic" that motivated the more overtly anti–Jewish polemicists of the late Middle Ages. Reuchlin believed that in the cabala, Jewish scholars had found a way to the hidden power of the Old Testament, and he regarded the Talmud as "the veiled Old Testament prophecy of the Messiah Jesus."[54]

On the sociopolitical level, Obermann shows that anti–Jewish polemics formed a key element in the various battles of the time. Polemical themes initially addressed against Jews were soon applied by reformers and Catholics to each other and by the popular pamphleteers against all of their perceived enemies, whether peasants or nobility. Thus, the anti–Judaism that evolved into anti–Semitism was woven into the fabric of modern society in its very development.

Luther's diatribes against the Jews and his advocacy of expulsion, destruction of synagogues, and prohibition of rabbinic teaching ironically represent a late flowering of the mendicant tradition sketched by Cohen. Anomalies, of course, persisted, reflecting the continued ambivalence of both Protestant and Catholic attitudes toward the Jews. While in Calvin's Geneva (as Yerushalmi reminds us), Jews were forbidden to reside, they were allowed to live in papal Rome (though in limited numbers). Yet Jews fleeing from the Inquisition in "Catholic" Spain and Portugal found refuge in the "Protestant" Netherlands. Though the reformers critically and effectively challenged many elements of their medieval heritage, anti–Jewishness was not, in the end, one of them.[55]

"Enlightened" Anti–Semitism: Hatred as Secular Ideology

The French Revolution and the Enlightenment brought about the emancipation of Jews from the ghetto. This period also removed the question of what now became the "Jewish problem" from the hands of Christian theory and put it in the hands, though no safer, of secular ideology. Until the publication of Arthur Hertzberg's revisionist study of the attitudes of the "enlightened" thinkers,[56] it commonly was assumed that the secularism of the Enlightenment was the best thing to happen to the Jews since the time of the Maccabees.[57] The treatment of the period in the *Encyclopedia Judaica* illustrates the current consensus of scholarship.[58]

The picture that emerges is of an anti–Semitism mutating with frightening ease to infect even the egalitarian reformers who brought about the emancipation of Jews from the ghettos. Some elements of the new strain of the disease continued from the Christian past, in effect secularizing older Christian attitudes. Many "enlightened" thinkers, for example, translated the Christian desire for Jewish conversion into a belief that Jews would lose their particularity by assimilation into the dominant, enlightened culture. Some, such as Diderot, were anti–Christians who sought to embarrass Christianity by demeaning its Jewish roots.

Others injected new and even more ominous elements into the strain. Voltaire, for example, saw Jews as a major threat to the progress of European culture and went so far as to imply that Jews were ignorant by their very nature and thus incapable of being integrated into society. The shift from the more traditional forms of Christian polemics, bad as they were, is significant. Christianity always held out to Jews the possibility of conversion and (with baptism) of full equality. Voltaire's implication, if carried out logically, would dehumanize the Jews to the point where by nature they were seen as beyond the pale of human fellowship itself.

Voltaire's essentially racist invectives did have a precedent in Catholic Spain in the period of the Counter-Reformation. The Spanish, worried about the Jewish taint in the lineage of so many of their leading families through intermarriage with *conversos* (converted Jews), developed the infamous "purity of blood" laws. These laws violated the basic principles of Christian theology and were rigorously opposed by such figures as St. Ignatius of Loyola and St. Teresa of Avila (herself descended from a judeo-converso family).

By the nineteenth century, Jews found themselves the victims of anti-Semitic abuse from many sides of the European ideological spectrum. To French ultraconservatives, including many clerics, the emancipation of Jews symbolized all that was despicable in modern liberalism. German nationalists viewed their non-Aryan character as a threat to the unification of the country. Radical secularists despised Jews for giving birth to Christianity, while, of course, the ancient teaching of contempt continued to be promoted by Protestant and Catholic preachers alike. Europe, religiously and ideologically divided, seemed to possess one point of unity: fear of the Jews, fear of their "differentness" and, perhaps, of the universal God to whom they witnessed. Fear, of course, easily turns into hatred to mask itself.

By the late nineteenth and early twentieth centuries, anti-Semitism was being widely exploited as a political tool. Czarist Russia, for example, concocted the infamous forgery, *The Protocols of the Elders of Zion*, to justify its pogroms. Houston Stewart Chamberlain, the son-in-law of Richard Wagner, based his popular racist philosophy upon it. In the welter of competing diatribes, curious anomalies of anti-Semitic demonology arose. One of the most enduring has been the self-contradictory image of the Jew as at once the arch-communist and the arch-capitalist. (Marx, after all, was Jewish, and "everybody knew" that Jews controlled all the world's banks). Nazism thus had a fertile field in which to sow its seeds of genocidal hatred. This field, ironically, was plowed by the Christian tradition of contempt for Judaism and by the secular ideologies that held Christianity itself in contempt. Some scholars have speculated that it was precisely in order to attack Christianity's roots that the secular venom of hatred was turned on the Jews.

John Pawlikowski surveys the range of current theological thinking in his monograph, *The Challenge of the Holocaust for Christian Theology*.[59] I shall not attempt to rework Pawlikowski's excellent treatise or enter into the debates outlined there, tempting as that may be. My task has been an historical one, not a theological one. I only hope that it will help to shed some light on the complexities of that history and therefore on the tasks facing Christian thought today.

Notes

1. Pope John Paul II, Address to Representatives of Catholic Bishop's Conference and Other Christian Churches, March 6, 1982, *National Catholic News Service* translation, March 17, 1982.

2. For an annotated bibliography of works up to 1976, see John T. Townsend in *The Study of Judaism Bibliographica Essays*, vol. 2 (New York: Anti-Defamation League, 1976). For works up to 1984, see Eugene J. Fisher, "A New Maturity in Christian-Jewish Dialogue: A Bibliographical Essay," *Face to Face* 11 (Spring 1984): 29–43.

3. See, for example, Bernard Doering, *Jacques Maritain and the French Catholic Intellectuals* (Notre Dame, Ind.: University Press, 1983), pp. 126–127. On the theological ambiguities that remained in the thought of both Protestant and Catholic thinkers at the time of the Holocaust, see Eugene J. Fisher, "Ani Ma'amin: Theological Responses to the Holocaust," *Interface* (National Conference of Catholic Bishops, Dec. 1980), pp. 1–8.

4. Jules Isaac, *Jesus and Israel*, trans. Claire Huchet Bishop (New York: Holt, Rinehart, Winston, 1971); and Jules Isaac, *The Teaching of Contempt*, trans. Claire Huchet Bishop (New York: Holt, Rinehart, Winston, 1964).

5. Gregory Baum, *Is the New Testament Anti-Semitic?*, rev. ed. (Mahwah, N.J.: Paulist Press, 1966), p. 15.

6. Ibid., p. 16.

7. It was a deceptively simple architecture at that. *The* Jews killed Jesus. Therefore, God became angry at them and destroyed the Temple, making them wander the face of the earth until they would acknowledge Jesus as Messiah.

8. Samuel Sandmel, *Anti-Semitism in the New Testament?* (Philadelphia: Fortress, 1978), p. 164. Sandmel's caveat on the importance of precision in language is also relevant to understanding the differing responses of scholars to the same historical material: "The nineteenth and twentieth century word *anti-Semitism* is a completely wrong term when transferred to the first and second Christian centuries....Scholars have proposed other terms: *Anti*-Jewish or *Anti-Judaism*. These terms are better because they are more correct; they simply have not caught on" (p. xxi).

9. Rosemary Radford Reuther, *Faith and Fratricide: The Theological Roots of Anti-Semitism* (New York: Seabury, Crossroad, 1974), p. 226.

10. "I have had to change my mind....The book I wrote in the late fifties and published in 1961 no longer represents my position on the relationship between Church and Synagogue" (Baum, in Reuther, *Faith and Fratricide*, pp. 3–4).

11. Sandmel, *Anti-Semitism in the New Testament?*, p. 164.

12. Alan T. Davies, ed., *Anti-Semitism and the Foundation of Christianity* (New York: Paulist Press, 1979), p. xv. Edward H. Flannery's recent revision of his classic, *The Anguish of the Jews: Twenty-three Centuries of Anti-Semitism* (New York: Macmillan, 1965; New York: Paulist Press, 1985), reveals an evolution of scholarly judgment similar to Baum's. The section on the New Testament in the 1965 edition concluded with a citation from Baum's 1961 text that "there is no foundation for the accusation that a seed of contempt and hatred for the Jews can be found in the New Testament" (p. 30). Yet Flannery's 1985 version, while distinguishing "theological anti-Judaism" and "negative prophetic statements delivered within a Jewish ambiance" from modern anti-Semitism, candidly acknowledges that the New Testament is "replete with an anti-Judaic theology and anti-Jewish pronouncement, prophetic in nature, that have made it a seedbed of anti-Semitism" (p. 33).

13. See, for example, Justin Martyr, *Dialogue with Trypho*; Epiphanius, *Haereses* 24.9; Jerome, *Commentary on Isaiah* (particularly his treatment of Is. 2:18, 49:7, 54:5).

14. John 9:22-35, 12:42, 16:2-3, cf. Acts 6-8.

15. Cf. Asher Finkel, "Yavneh's Liturgy and Early Christianity," *Journal of Ecumenical Studies* 18, no. 2 (Spring 1981): 231-250; Reuven Kimelman, "Birkat Ha-minim and the Lack of Evidence for an Anti-Christian Prayer in Late Antiquity," in *Jewish and Christian Self-Definition,* ed. E.P. Sanders (Philadelphia: Fortress, 1981); Steven T. Katz, "Issues in the Separation of Judaism and Christianity," *Journal of Biblical Literature* 103 (1984): 43-76.

16. For example, Charles Journet, *Destinee d'Israel* (Paris: Egloff, 1945). "Yahweh himself, in choosing the Jews as a unique messianic and theophoric people, would...design them for the hostility of the world and pagan peoples, long before the Incarnation, long before the deicide. In Egypt in the thirteenth century and in Persia in the fifth before Christ, the pogrom is already there" (pp. 199-200).

17. Salo W. Baron, *A Social and Religious History of the Jews,* vol. 1 (New York: Columbia University Press, 1951), p. 194.

18. Marcel Simon, *Verus Israel* (Paris: de Boccard, 1948), p. 263. Edward Flannery, commenting on this passage, notes that Simon "imputes this tendency" to James Parkes, J. Juster, and, in his 1965 edition of *The Anguish of the Jews,* to Jules Isaac (p. 491). Flannery himself adds Leon Poliakov (cf. Edward H. Flannery, *The Anguish of the Jews,* 1965, p. 281). In the 1985 edition of *Anguish,* Flannery again revises an earlier view. Where the 1965 edition gave "first place" among the "sources of Christian anti-Semitism" to the pagan anti-Semitism that converts brought with them to the Church (p.61), the 1985 edition reduces this to a "secondary cause." Flannery states frankly that "the principal source of Christian anti-Semitism was the Church's theological anti-Judaism" (p. 62).

19. Flannery, *Anguish*, 1965 edition, p. 281. References are to the 1965 edition unless otherwise noted.

20. F. Lovksy, *Antisemitisme et mystere d'Israel* (Paris: Michel, 1955), p. 45.

21. Flannery, *Anguish*, pp. 3–43.

22. Reuther, *Faith and Fratricide*, p. 27.

23. Robert L. Wilken, *John Chrysostum and the Jews: Rhetoric and Reality in the Late Fourth Century* (Berkeley and Los Angeles: University of California Press, 1983).

24. Ibid., p. 163.

25. For a discussion of the literature on medieval developments in anti-Semitism, see the section on "Medieval Christianity: A New State in Anti-Semitism" later in this essay.

26. Wilken, *Chrysostum and the Jews*, p. 163. The notion of theological significance for the destruction of the Temple, of course, is a theme already present in the New Testament, most obviously in the Epistle to the Hebrews.

27. Gregory Baum, "Catholic Dogma After Auschwitz" in Davies, *Foundation of Christianity*, pp. 140–141.

28. Raymond Brown, cited in Eugene J. Fisher, *Seminary Education and Christian–Jewish Relations* (Washington, D.C.: National Catholic Education Association, 1983), p. 38.

29. John G. Gager, *The Origins of Anti–Semitism: Attitudes toward Judaism in Pagan and Christian Antiquity* (New York: Oxford University Press, 1983), p. 25.

30. Gager, *Origins of Anti–Semitism*, pp. 141–153.

31. Ibid., p. 183.

32. Ibid., p. 159.

33. See Krister Stendahl, *Paul among the Jews and Gentiles* (Philadelphia: Fortress, 1976). Franz Mussner, *Tractate on the Jews: The Significance of Judaism for the Christian Faith*, tr. Leonard Swidler (Philadelphia: Fortress, 1984); John Koenig, *Jews and Christians in Dialogue: New Testament Foundations* (Philadelphia: Westminster Press, 1979); and E.P. Sanders, *Paul, the Law and the Jewish People* (Philadelphia: Fortress, 1983).

34. Gager, *Origins of Anti–Semitism*, p. 202.

35. Ibid., p. 247.

36. Part of the difficulty of classification is that Gager studiously ignores the classic division of most of the literature into treatments of "canonical and non–canonical books," arguing that the distinction is valid only from a post facto theological point of view and merely obscures the complex reality of the period of early Christianity as a whole (ibid., p. 33). Thus, his principle of organization differs from that chosen for this essay.

37. Ibid., p. 9. Interestingly, a similar sort of statement recently has been made by Mark Saperstein concerning the presumption of

universal anti-Semitism among Christians in the medieval period in his introduction to the republication of Joshua Trachtenberg's classic, *The Devil and the Jews* (New Haven: Yale University Press, 1943; New York: Anti-Defamation League, 1983). Contemporary scholarship, after passing through a period necessarily confronting honestly and acknowledging the deep-seated character of anti-Jewishness in Western history, is now reclaiming a sense of balance in which that negative history is seen in a wider (if more ambiguous) context. This, it appears to me, is a healthy development, so long as the tragedies of the past are not once again swept under the historical rug.

38. Menahem Stern and Shimon Applebaum, cited in Gager, *Origins of Anti-Semitism*, p. 36.

39. See George Foote Moore, "Christian Writers on Judaism," *Harvard Theological Review* 14 (1921): 197–254; Charlotte Klein, *Anti-Judaism in Christian Theology* (Philadelphia: Fortress, 1978); and E.P. Sanders, *Paul and Palestinian Judaism* (Philadelphia: Fortress, 1977); cf. also Solomon Schecter, "Higher Criticism—Higher Anti-Semitism," in *Seminary Addresses and Other Papers* (Cincinnati: Hebrew Union College, 1915).

40. Gager, *Origins of Anti-Semitism*, p. 32.

41. Ibid.

42. Ibid., pp. 32–33. Cf. Moore, "Christian Writers," pp. 23–24; Sanders, *Paul and Palestinian Judaism*, p. 52; Stendahl, "Judaism and Christianity: A Plea for a New Relationship," *Cross Currents* 17 (1967): 455–458; Klein, *Anti-Judaism*, p. 4.

43. Cf. Eugene J. Fisher, "From Polemic to Objectivity: The Use and Abuse of Hebrew Sources in New Testament Scholarship," *Hebrew Studies and Journal* 20–21 (Fall 1980): 199–208.

44. The papers are collected in Eva Fleischner, ed., *Auschwitz: Beginning of a New Era? Reflections on the Holocaust* (Hoboken, N.J.: Ktav, 1977).

45. Yosef Hayim Yerushalmi, "Response to Rosemary Reuther," in Fleischner, *Auschwitz: Beginning of a New Era?*, p. 98.

46. Ibid., pp 99–101.

47. On the development of medieval canon law regarding Jews and Judaism, see Edward Synan, *The Popes and the Jews in the Middle Ages* (New York: Macmillan, 1965). Throughout, Synan stresses the theoretical ambivalence of Christianity's theological and hence practical attitudes toward the Jews in its midst.

48. Yerushalmi, "Response to Reuther," p. 102.

49. Ibid., p. 103.

50. Jeremy Cohen, *The Friars and the Jews: The Evolution of Medieval Anti-Judaism* (Ithaca, N.Y.: Cornell University Press, 1983).

51. Augustine, *De civitate Dei* 18:46; cf. 20:29 and *Tractatus adversus judeos*, in J.-P. Migne, *Patrologia Latina* (Paris, 1844) 42:51–67, as cited in Cohen, *The Friars and the Jews*, pp. 20–21.

52. Cohen, *The Friars and the Jews*, p. 244.

53. Heiko Obermann, *Roots of Anti-Semitism in the Age of Renaissance and Reformation* (Philadelphia: Fortress, 1984).

54. Ibid., p. 12.

55. Protestant scholar A. Roy Eckardt, "The Mutual Plight of the Churches," in his collection, *Your People, My People* (New York: Quadrangle, 1974), pp. 68–77, comments that "Protestantism, Catholicism, and Orthodox Christianity share the one predicament respecting the Jewish people and Judaism," arguing that "Protestant reformers retained the traditional Christian position of hostility toward Jews" (p. 21).

56. Arthur Hertzberg, *The French Enlightenment and the Jews* (New York: Columbia University, 1968).

57. This statement is an oversimplification, of course. It is not, I think, without merit as a thumbnail sketch of at least the prevailing attitude of the *Wissenschaff des Jedentuums* movement and those scholars trained under its influence.

58. Cf. Yizhak Heinemann et al., *Anti-Semitism*, Israel Pocket Library (Jerusalem: Keter, 1974), pp. 24–39. Authors listed for the section include, along with Hertzberg, Heinemann, Joshua Gutmann, Leon Poliakov, Paul Weissman, Yehoshafat Harkabi, and Binyamin Eliav.

59. John Pawlikowski, *The Challenge of the Holocaust for Christian Theology* (New York: Anti-Defamation League, 1976, revised 1983).

Chapter 2

Luther and the Roots of the Holocaust

Richard L. Rubenstein

1983 marked the five hundredth anniversary of the birth of Martin Luther. Only nine years old when Columbus discovered the New World, Luther did as much to discover the new world of the spirit as Columbus did to discover the territorial New World. If, as many historians and sociologists of religion maintain, the modern world is in large measure an unintended consequence of religious and cultural forces arising out of the Protestant Reformation, Luther can be seen as one of its primary creators. We can, however, inquire concerning the extent to which the great reformer contributed to one of the darker aspects of modernity, anti–Semitic genocide.

According to Ernst Troeltsch, the new element in the Protestant theology initiated by Luther was "the special content of the conception of grace."[1] Before Luther, grace was regarded as a mystical reality imparted through the sacraments. Protestantism came to regard grace as "a Divine temper of faith, conviction, spirit, knowledge, and trust...discerned as the loving will of God which brings about forgiveness of sins."[2] As a consequence, according to Troeltsch, religion became essentially a matter of faith and conviction. This development was of enormous importance, as we shall see, in shaping Luther's attitude towards the Jews. By putting the whole weight of his religious commitment on faith, it became supremely important for Luther to discredit any group that might challenge his system of beliefs. It was the unfortunate destiny of the Jews to challenge, simply by fidelity to their own tradition, what was absolutely fundamental to Luther, his reading of Scripture.[3]

Troeltsch points out that the Reformation involved a "reduction of the whole of religion to that which alone can be an object of faith and trust, that is, to that idea of God...which represents Him as a gracious Will, holy, forgiving sins."[4] Thus a crucial element in the Protestant Reformation involved the truncation of religion from an all–embracing system of rite, belief, and culture to a system of faith and conviction. More than any of his predecessors, Luther based his religious commitment on faith. Troeltsch has commented that

Luther's concentration on faith as the decisive element in religion constituted "an enormous simplification in doctrine."[5]

Luther was convinced that no institution or body of ritual could enable natural man to ascend to the supernatural. Without intervention from beyond nature, no human institution, not even the Church, could rescue man from the fate that awaits all creatures. Thus, for Luther, man immersed in nature without God is hopelessly lost. No atheistic existentialist ever held a bleaker image of the human condition than this. Luther once commented that he would rather be a sow than a man without Christ, because a sow does not have the fear and the anxiety to which natural man is condemned after the Fall.

It was Luther's unique contribution to the religious thought of his time to insist that, though man's fallen nature hopelessly cuts him off from God, nevertheless, the grace and righteousness of God allows sinful man reconciliation. However, such a reconciliation is entirely dependent on what God does, not what man does. Moreover, the good news whereby we learn of this reconciliation can be found solely in Scripture, where the central message and true meaning is God's justification of man in and through Christ.

Notice what has transpired: Luther has abandoned the medieval hope that man can rise from nature to supernature through this-worldly means, whether religion or reason. Everything now depends upon the truth of Scripture's account of God's promises. Luther tells us that "Christians are assured that Christ is the ruling Messiah." He then adds, "If this were not so, then God's word and promise would be a lie."[6] For Luther and those who follow him, if his reading of Scripture is without foundation, there is no hope of human salvation. Yet, it was precisely Luther's reading of Scripture that was challenged not only by Jews but by many Christians as well. Some way had to be found to meet the challenge.

I believe that Luther's "enormous simplification of doctrine," to use Troeltsch's phrase, significantly aggravated the hazard of Jews domiciled in regions under his influence. Perhaps this can be understood better by using a little imagination. Let's say that in the year 1540, three years before Luther wrote his most violently anti–Jewish work, *On the Jews and Their Lies*, a delegation of Chinese living in Saxony began discussions with the great reformer. Had Luther told this imaginary delegation of his faith in redemption through Christ as revealed in the Gospels, its members might have responded, "Dr. Luther, we really don't know what you are talking about. We know about Enlightenment, and we know about the cycle of dependent causation. But we do not know about your Christ, nor do we know anything about the God you say speaks to men through your holy books."

No doubt Luther would have been disturbed and annoyed, but his displeasure could hardly have been remotely as strong as was his annoyance with the Jews. We need not conjecture on this subject. Luther published *On the Jews and Their Lies* in response to an actual Jewish challenge to his interpretation of Scripture,[7] a letter he had received from Count Wolf Schlick zu Falkenau that enclosed a polemic by a rabbi against Luther's 1538 work, *Against the Sabbatarians*. The count requested that Luther answer the rabbinical treatise (which is no longer extant). Thus, Luther's most important and most hostile anti–Jewish document was written in response to a Jewish challenge and as a defense of his own reading of Scripture.

Of course, Luther was far more hostile to the Jews than he would have been to the Chinese for a very important reason. Unlike the Chinese, the Jews agreed with Luther that God was the ultimate source of Scripture's authority. Both Luther and the Jews regarded the human condition as fallen and in need of divine redemption. There was, however, an unbridgeable gap in their understanding of how redemption was to take place. For the Jews, redemption ultimately would come about through compliance with the will of God as revealed in Scripture and as interpreted by the rabbis. For Luther, the Jewish belief was not only mistaken but perverse and demonic. To rely upon human works, such as the corpus of Jewish religious practice, was to make precisely the kind of spiritual error that had been fostered by the Catholic Church in its insistence that the sacraments were the path to salvation. Moreover, the Jewish error was compounded by rejection of Christ as Redeemer. Thus, the Jews were far more offensive to Luther than any other religious community. Having reduced all of Christian hope to a scripturally based faith in Jesus Christ, Luther could hardly be expected to look kindly upon proponents of a tradition that used Scripture to deny Luther's sole assurance of salvation. If the Jews were right, Luther had nothing to hope for, save the sow's fate and absent the sow's blessed ignorance.

By contrast, Judaism posed far less of a challenge to Roman Catholicism than it did to Luther, simply because of the strength of religion, culture, and tradition that stood under the medieval Church. Jews may have challenged some aspects of Catholic belief in the Middle Ages, but they were in no position to challenge the imposing edifice of medieval Christian civlization as a whole. Ironically, when Luther reduced the religious foundations of Christianity to faith in Christ as revealed in Scripture, he added greater weight to the Jewish challenge and thus to the Jewish danger. Not only had Luther reduced religious hope to a single source, the Bible, but he had chosen the one source the Jews were best able to challenge. Jewish scholars were at home in their ancestral language, the language of Scripture, and they were the people into whose midst Jesus of Nazareth had been born.

Luther began *On the Jews and Their Lies* by stating that the interpretation of Scripture was the fundamental area of conflict between him and the Jews. "I have received a treatise in which a Jew engages in a dialogue with a Christian," he wrote. Luther complained that the Jewish author "dares to pervert the Scriptural passages which we cite in the testimony to our faith, concerning our Lord Jesus Christ and Mary his mother, and to interpret them quite differently. With this argument he thinks he can destroy the basis of our faith."[9] A very large part of *On the Jews and Their Lies* is given over to Luther's refutation of the Jewish interpretation of Scripture. Moreover, Luther was altogether clear concerning what was at stake in this dispute: if the Jewish interpretation is correct, Christian faith in Christ's redemption is without foundation. Luther's fundamental motive for his attack is thus the defense of his reading of Christian faith.

In the treatise, Luther asserts that he is neither interested in quarreling with the Jews nor in attempting to convert them. Whatever hopes he may have had at an earlier period for their conversion have long since been abandoned. "They have," he writes, "failed to learn any lesson from the terrible distress that has been theirs for over fourteen hundred years in exile."[10] Nevertheless, Luther counseled those Christians who have reason to enter into dialogue with Jews to offer their religious rivals the following proof of their errors:

> But if you have to or want to talk to them, do not say any more than this: "Listen Jew, are you aware that Jerusalem and your sovereignty, together with your priesthood, have been destroyed for over 1460 years...." Let the Jew bite on this nut and dispute this question as long as they wish.
>
> *For such ruthless wrath of God is sufficient evidence that they have erred and gone astray....*For one dare not regard God as so cruel that he would punish his own people so long, so terribly, so unmercifully, and in addition keep silent, comforting them neither with words nor with deeds, and fixing no time limit and no end to it. Who would have faith, hope, or love towards such a God? Therefore this work of wrath is proof that the Jews, surely rejected by God, are no longer his people, and neither is he any longer their God.
>
> In short, as I have already said, do not engage much in debate with Jews about articles of faith....*There is no hope in them until they reach the point where their misery finally makes them so pliable that they are forced to confess that the Messiah has come and he is our Jesus.*[11] (Italics added.)

For Luther, like many Christian thinkers both ancient and modern, the best refutation of the Jewish reading of Scripture is Jewish misfortune. Luther's argument differs little from that of the prophets, except that the prophets lovingly admonished their own community, whereas Luther displays no love in his description of those he regards as enemies and strangers. Basically, he says, had the Jews understood God's revelation and conformed to his will, none of their terrible sufferings would have taken place. Luther argues that a just God would never have visited so horrible a fate on any people, much less the people of the original covenant. Luther sees only one hope for the Jews: their fate will become so replete with misery that a few will see the light and accept Christ as their Savior.

We cannot doubt how Luther would have interpreted the Holocaust: he would have seen it as decisive proof of God's rejection of the Jews. Not surprisingly, when German Lutheran theologians met in Darmstadt in 1948, three years after the Holocaust, they proclaimed that the Holocaust was a divine punishment and called upon the Jews to halt their rejection and ongoing crucifixion of Christ.[12] Whatever their motives in issuing such a statement, the modern theologians undoubtedly spoke in the spirit of the founder of their church.

Although Luther's arguments are harsh and although contemporary Lutherans, at least in North America, have tended to disassociate themselves from the overtly anti–Semitic aspects of his writings, we must recognize that his position regarding Judaism conforms to the classical position of Christianity. Luther explicitly derives his position that Jewish misfortune is proof of Christian truth and Jewish error from Scripture:

Well, let the Jews regard our Lord Jesus Christ as they will. We behold the fulfillment of the words spoken by him in Luke 21:22f.:

"But when you see Jerusalem surrounded by armies, then know that its desolation has come near....for these are days of vengeance.

"For great distress shall be upon the earth and wrath upon this people."[13]

Moreover, I must sadly observe that Luther's polemical use of history to discredit the Jewish interpretation of Scripture was by no means without a measure of methodological justification. Both Judaism and Christianity traditionally have claimed exclusive knowledge of God's revelation. The Jewish–Christian controversy fundamentally was concerned with the historical question of what God did in his relations with Israel and, through Israel, to all of humanity. Jews could hardly expect that their rabbis could publicly reject the Christian view of God's action in history without receiving a Christian response, especially in the case of Martin Luther. Since he depended on Scripture as the sole source of revealed truth, it was inevitable that he would argue from history to discredit Judaism. For Luther to have taken the secular view that honorable men can sincerely disagree on such questions would have shaken the very foundation upon which rested his hope for redemption.

Unfortunately, Luther's theologically inevitable polemic led to defamation of Judaism, by Luther as well as other Christian leaders, in terms more radical than any used before to discredit a rival religious community. The Jews and their religion, in Luther's eyes, are the incarnation of radical evil. For Luther, the Jews are of the devil. And Luther's devil was a real rather than a metaphorical power. Here are some characteristic expressions of the reformer's opinions on the subject:

> I advise you not to enter their synagogues: all devils might dismember and devour you there....For he who cannot hear or bear to hear God's word is not of God's people. And if they are not God's people, then they are the devil's people.[14]

> You cannot learn from them anything except how to misunderstand the divine commandments....Therefore be on your guard against the Jews, knowing that wherever they have their synagogues, nothing is found but a den of devils in which....blasphemy and defaming of God and men are practiced most maliciously.[15]

Elsewhere, Luther expresses himself in a similar vein:

> They are real liars and bloodhounds.... Their heart's most ardent...yearning...is set on the day on which they can deal with us Gentiles as they did with the Gentiles in Persia at the time of Esther....The sun has never shone on a more bloodthirsty and vengeful people than they are who imagine that they are God's people who have been commissioned and commanded to murder and to slay the Gentiles. In fact, the most important thing that they expect of their Messiah is that he will murder and kill the entire world with their sword.[16]

In the late nineteenth and early twentieth centuries, a forged document, *The Protocols of the Elders of Zion*, was circulated widely and accorded credibility especially throughout Europe between the wars. In it, Jewish leaders were depicted as secretly plotting world domination. Historians of the Holocaust have maintained that this document provided anti-Semites with a "warrant for genocide."[17] *The Protocals'* distribution contributed to a climate in which the extermination of the Jews was believed beneficial by large sectors of Europe's population. Nevertheless, even the *Protocols* did not go as far as Luther did when he accused the Jews of plotting genocide against the Gentile world. Not content with verbal aggression, Luther actively sought the expulsion of the Jews from Saxony, an effort that succeeded in 1536. When the edict was partly rescinded two years later, Luther vehemently opposed the action. Even in his last sermon, preached on February 15, 1546, three days before his death, Luther demanded the expulsion of the Jews from Germany.

In other instances, Luther was not above advocating overt violence against the Jews and their institutions. Consider the following excerpts from his writing:

We are at fault in not slaying them. Rather we allow
them to live freely in our midst despite all their murdering,
cursing, blaspheming, lying, and defaming....
What shall we Christians do with this rejected and condemned people, the Jews? Since they live among us, we dare
not tolerate their conduct, now that we are aware of their
lying and reviling and blaspheming....
First, to set fire to their synagogues or schools and to
bury and cover with dirt whatever will not burn, so that no
man will ever again see a stone or a cinder of them. This is to
be done in honor of our Lord and of Christendom, so that
God might see that we are Christians, and do not condone or
knowingly tolerate such public lying, cursing, and blaspheming of his Son and of his Christians....
In Deuteronomy 13:12ff. Moses writes that any city that
is given over to idolatry shall be totally destroyed by fire, and
nothing of it shall be preserved. If he were alive today, he
could be the first to set fire to the synagogues and the houses
of the Jews....
Secondly, I advise that their houses also be razed. For
they pursue in them the same aims as in their synagogues.[19]
(Italics added.)

Luther continues at length in much the same spirit, but we have little
need to follow him any further. Interestingly, the editor of the American translation of Luther's works comments about this passage:

It is impossible to publish Luther's treatise today...without
noting how similar to his proposals were the actions of the
National Socialist regime in the 1930's and 1940's. On the
night of November 9–10, 1938, the so-called *Kristallnacht*,
for example, 119 symagogues in all parts of Germany, together with many Jewish homes and shops, were burned to
the ground....In subsequently undertaking the physical annihilation of the Jews, however, the Nazis surpassed even
Luther's severity.[20]

Although he obviously is disturbed by Luther's call to overt violence,
especially in view of the events of World War II, the editor apparently has overlooked the beginning of this passage where Luther
writes, "We are at fault in not slaying them."

What shall we make of this religiously legitimized incitement to
homicidal violence? For many Jews, passages such as this provide
evidence of a moral flaw in the nature of Christianity and, especially,
in the stature of Luther. Many post–Holocaust Christians, including
members and leaders of Lutheran churches, find the passages acutely
embarrassing. We must recall, however, that in the 1930s, *On the
Jews and Their Lies* occasioned little embarrassment in German Lutheran circles. When the 1936 edition of the treatise was published in

Munich, the editor claimed approvingly that *On the Jews and Their Lies* was the arsenal from which anti–Semitism had drawn its weapons.[21] Other German Lutheran leaders of the period, including Bishop Otto Dibelius, who was to serve as president of the World Council of Churches in 1965, saw the National Socialist policies towards the Jews as the fulfillment of Luther's program.[22] Of all European churches from 1933 to 1945, none was as silent or as indifferent to the known fate of the Jews—when it did not actively support National Socialist anti–Semitic policies—as was the German Lutheran church.

However one views his writings on the Jews, Luther was undeniably one of the most influential religious leaders of all time. The sheer violence of the position taken by so overwhelmingly important a figure points to a significant, though often neglected, aspect of Christian anti–Judaism: the crucial question is not why mean–spirited or malicious people were so violently anti–Jewish, but why some of the greatest thinkers and most pious saints within Christianity adopted such a posture.

Apparently, Luther, and others like him, felt compelled to negate and discredit the disconfirming other in order to maintain the credibility of his fundmental religious beliefs and values. And because of the shared scriptural inheritance of Judaism and Christianity, the Jew is Christianity's disconfirming other *par excellence,* as the Christian is the same for Judaism.

Luther's need to discredit the disconfirming other can best be understood in terms of the social–psychological theory of cognitive dissonance, which holds that if a person or a group has an important stake in an item of information that does not fit together psychologically with a second item of information, an attempt at making the dissonant items consistent with each other will be undertaken. This process, known as dissonance reduction,[23] might seek obvious recourse by discrediting the source of the dissonant information. An even more radical method would be to eliminate the source entirely. Both methods have been employed in the history of religion. Nevertheless, the basic motive for even the most abusive attempts at dissonance reduction is defense of values or beliefs that are perceived to be indispensable to the survival of one's own community.

The related problems of dissonance reduction and the presence of the disconfirming other were especially urgent for Luther because of the overwhelming importance his distinctive reading of Scripture held for his religious system. As noted above, if that reading proved mistaken, nothing was left. Luther thus had little option but to attempt to convince, discredit, or eliminate the Jew as disconfirming other. To convince meant to seek to convert; to discredit involved religious defamation such as the canard that the Jews were incarnations of the devil; to eliminate meant expulsion or mass murder. At the very least, Luther was compelled to defame the Jews and Judaism to minimize the credibility of their reading of Scripture and for their failure to accept Jesus as the Messiah. As a practical consequence of being discredited or eliminated, the disconfirming other faces the danger of becoming wholly alien, that is, wholly outside of the universe of moral obligation of those whose values are challenged. When, as in the case of the Jews, the other is identified with the devil, any conceivable violence, even extermination camps, are in effect religiously legitimized.

Keep in mind, however, that Luther's attack on the Jews is not an isolated phenomenon. It arises out of the monotheistic exclusivism common to all of the religious traditions rooted in the Bible. For practical reasons, the exclusivity can be softened and played down, but each of the biblical traditions contains the seeds of a resurgence of intolerance and violence on the part of those who claim that they are defending the true meaning of their tradition. The exclusivity is grounded in Scripture. Admittedly, Scripture can be interpreted so as to minimize the problem. But there does not seem to be any way to eliminate the component of exclusivity altogether. Neither Protestantism, nor Roman Catholicism, nor Judaism, nor Islam appears able to wholly abandon the claim that it alone is the true faith.

In a complex, interdependent world, one hopes there are better solutions to this problem. Yet, we had better be warned by Luther's example. In times of minimal social stress, exclusive religions can live in relative peace with one another, especially when relations among them are clearly defined. Unfortunately, we have seen too many examples of periods of heightened social stress during which religious and communal strife intensify to the point of large–scale violence. The Reformation was such a time. So too was World War II. Moreover, such violence has all too frequently received religious legitimation. Luther's demonization of the Jews and Judaism in the sixteenth century, which in its turn reiterated the view of the Jews found in the Gospels, gave sacred sanction in the twentieth century to a view of the Jews as enemies wholly outside any conceivable German universe of moral obligation. It is hardly surprising that not a single German church group protested the stripping of Jewish rights to citizenship, the forced deportation to the east of Jews whose families had lived in Germany for centuries, or the widely known, state–sponsored, systematic extermination of Europe's Jewish population. And Germany was by no means the only country without effective religious protest against the extermination project.

Though Luther was hardly original in his virulent demonization of the Jews, he nevertheless made the Bible available to Germans in their native tongue and did more to shape the religious life of his nation than any other figure in German history. He did not create the gas chambers. He did, however, contribute significantly to their indispensable precondition, the denial of the Jews' humanity and their transformation into Satan's spawn. His contribution to the Holocaust is made especially ironic by the nature of his motives. Luther's overriding interest was the defense of Christian faith. It was the historic misfortune of the Jews that their religious civilization challenged that faith. This did not automatically make them candidates for the gas chambers. Yet it did result in legitimizing their treatment as satanic nonpersons to whom the German Christians were bound by no moral obligation whatsoever.

Hitler's public notice of his intention to exterminate the Jews remains a matter of scholarly debate. In any event, it cannot have been later than his Reichstag speech of January 30, 1939, where he proclaimed to the world, "If international Jewry should succeed, in Europe or elsewhere, in precipitating nations into a world war, the result will not be the bolshevization of Europe and a victory for Judaism, *but the extermination in Europe of the Jewish race*" (italics added). In the winter of 1939, only Hitler and the National Socialists desired and were preparing for war. Translated into the language of the real world, Hitler in effect was saying, "I intend to go to war, and before it is over, I intend to exterminate the Jews of Europe."

As it became obvious that this was the one promise Hitler intended to keep, German Lutheranism was neither able nor, apparently, even interested in defining such mass destruction as morally out of bounds. As noted above, even three years after the war, German Lutheran theologians could not keep silent in the face of the monumental tragedy, but felt compelled to proclaim the Holocaust as God's punishment of the people who continued to crucify Christ. The danger inherent in the Jewish challenge to Luther's interpretation of Scripture was not fully apparent until World War II.

Notes

1. Ernst Troeltsch, *The Social Teaching of the Christian Churches*, trans. Olive Wyon, vol. 2 (New York: Macmillan, 1950), p. 468. On Luther's life and thought, see Heiko A. Obermann, *Luther: Mensch Zwichen Gott und Teufel* (Berlin: 1982).

2. Troeltsch, *Social Teaching*, vol. 2, p. 469.

3. Heiko A. Obermann, *Wurzeln des Antisemitismus: Christenangst und Judenplage in Zeitalter von Humanismus und Reformation* (Berlin: Severin und Siedler, 1981).

4. Troeltsch, *Social Teaching*, p. 469.

5. Ibid., p. 470

6. Martin Luther, *On the Jews and Their Lies*, trans. Martin H. Bertram, in *Luther's Works: The Christian in Society IV*, vol. 47 (Philadelphia: Fortress, 1957), p. 192.

7. See Walter Bienert, *Martin Luther und die Juden: Ein Quellenbuch mit Zeitgenossischen Illustrationen, mit Einfuhrungen und*

Erlauterungen (Frankfurt am Main: Evangelisches Verlagswerk, 1982), pp. 130 ff.

8. Ibid., p. 130.

9. Luther, *On the Jews*, p. 137.

10. Ibid., p. 138.

11. Ibid., pp. 138–139.

12. "*Ein Wort zur Judenfrage, der Reichbruderrat der Evangelischen Kirche in Deutschland,*" April 8, 1948, in Dietrich Goldschmidt and Hans–Joachim Kraus, eds., *Der Ungekundigte Bund: Neue Bewegung von Judischen and Christlicher* (Stuttgart: 1962), pp. 251–254.

13. Luther, *On the Jews*, p. 139.

14. Ibid., p. 154.

15. Ibid., p. 172.

16. Ibid., pp. 156–157. See also Esther 9:5 ff.

17. See Norman Cohn, *Warrant for Genocide: The Myth of the Jewish World—Conspiracy and the Protocols of the Elders of Zion* (New York: Harper and Row, 1969).

18. Bienert, *Martin Luther und die Juden*, pp. 174–177.

19. Luther, *On the Jews*, pp. 267–269.

20. Ibid., p. 268, n. 173.

21. H.H. Borchert and Georg Merz, eds., *Martin Luther: Ausgewahlte Werke,* vol. 3 (Munchen: 1936), pp. 61 ff. See Aarne Siirala, "Reflections from a Lutheran Perspective," in Eva Fleischner, ed., *Auschwitz: Beginning of a New Era? Reflections on the Holocaust* (New York: K'tav, 1974), pp. 135–148.

22. See John Conway, *The Nazi Persecution of the Churches: 1933–45* (New York: Basic Books, 1968), pp. 1–44 and 261–267; on Dibelius, p. 4ll.

23. On the theory of cognitive dissonance, see Leon Festinger, "Cognitive Dissonance," *Scientific American*, October 1962; Leon Festinger, Henry W. Riecken, and Stanley Schacter, *When Prophecy Fails* (Evanston, Ill.: Row and Peterson, 1957).

Chapter 3

Why People Kill:
Conditions for Participation in Mass Murder

Herbert Hirsch

"So you didn't feel they were human beings?"
"Cargo....They were cargo."
"There were so many children, did they ever make you think of your children, of how you would feel in the position of those parents?"
"No...I can't say I ever thought this way....You see...I rarely saw them as individuals. It was always as a huge mass."

Gitta Sereny, interviewing Franz Stangl, Commandant of Sobibor and Treblinka extermination camps, *Into That Darkness*

The large–scale destruction of human life is not a new phenomenon nor an old one. It has been observed throughout history and remains very much a part of contemporary life. Elie Wiesel puts it eloquently in *One Generation After* when he tells us why the search for understanding must never be abandoned. Society, he notes, has changed little:

if so many strategists are preparing the explosion of the planet and so many people willingly submit, if so many men still live under oppression and so many others in indifference, only one conclusion is possible; namely, that the failure of the black years has begotten yet another failure. Nothing has been learned; Auschwitz has not even served as warning. For more detailed information, consult your daily newspaper.[1]

When we, as scholars and human beings, attempt to probe the complete evil of events such as Auschwitz and Treblinka, we often find ourselves enveloped in a deep, disturbing silence: the mass destruction of men, women, and children is beyond explanation.[2] To label mass murder inexplicable seems to me a form of escape. Acts that seem beyond human capability should not be allowed to remain un-

A version of this chapter appeared in *The International Journal of Group Tensions*, 1985, Volume 15, Number 1-4, pp. 41-57.

examined. As individual human beings, we have to try, in the tradition of Holocaust scholarship, to understand why these events occur.

We must begin with the realization that mass murder does not occur in a vacuum. For people to die, other people have to pull the triggers, release the gases, and drop the bombs. Our search for understanding might begin with a consideration of Raul Hilberg's classic work, *The Destruction of the European Jews.*

Hilberg notes that in order for mass murder to proceed, mechanisms must be developed to short–circuit traditional concepts of individual morality. Psychologically, people must not be allowed to feel guilt when they destroy others. (Lifton refers to a similar phenomenon as psychic numbing.[3]) Guilt, from this perspective, is an interesting and important concept. One writer has observed that there are at least two forms of guilt: the personal feelings of the actors and the formal pronouncement by the state.[4] Of course, these are not mutually exclusive. Feelings of guilt may be brought on by commission of acts regarded as immoral or illegal. Actually, this breaks down into externally defined guilt and internally defined guilt and a mutual and dialectical relationship between the two.

Interesting as these concepts may be, of immediate interest here are the conditions that allow mass murder to take place without any guilt manifested at all, whether or not it is present. In short, what are the conditions for what Troy Duster has called "guilt–free massacre."[5] In his original presentation, six conditions are discussed. I have narrowed them to three broader, more inclusive categories—essentially, three conditions for guilt–free massacre. Lacking more adequate descriptive terminology, I call them the cultural, psychological, and political conditions.

Cultural Conditions

Perhaps the most general of the three, the cultural conditions usually are tied to the myths and ideologies stressed in a culture or nation state.[6] Every society claims a genealogy, a point of origin grounded in myth that explains the birth of its people or of the nation state. Generally, these myths hold that the members of the group or the state descend from divine sources or are protected by divine intervention. In the case of groups of people, the group is said to descend from God or gods or from some mythic hero or animal. In the case of the state, interpretation of the founding may be based on divine intervention resulting in divine protection. Both cases represent rudimentary types of historical thinking which function to differentiate the group or state from other groups or states and to invest the actions of the state or group with a legitimacy beyond that normally accorded the actions of human beings. After all, if you are descended from or inspired and protected by gods, your actions, because they are not merely human acts, cannot be questioned.

Historical examples are not difficult to come by. The Nazis invoked the ideas of blood and soil in their myth. They wanted to appeal to pre-Christian times to justify their superiority and to rationalize the "final solution."[7] The picture of the Jew drawn by Nazi propaganda was not new. It was part of a cultural legacy that had developed and had been drawn, in fact, several hundred years before by Martin Luther. In *On the Jews and Their Lies*, Luther had written:

Herewith you can readily see how they understand and obey the fifth commandment of God, namely that they are thirsty bloodhounds and murderers of all Christiandom, with full intent, now for more than fourteen hundred years, and indeed they were often burned to death upon the accusation that they had poisoned the water and wells, stolen children, and torn and hacked them apart, in order to cool their temper secretly with Christian blood.[8]

Luther's portrait of the Jew became a well-known part of anti-Semitic rhetoric. First, it claimed that Jews wished to rule the world; second, they were archcriminals, killers of Christ and all Christendom; third, they were a "plague, pestilence and pure misfortune."[9] This picture remained somewhat constant in anti-Semitic propaganda and mythology and was part of the Nazi myth articulated by Hitler. "The Jew," he stated, "completely lacks the most essential prerequisite of a cultural people....He is and remains a parasite, a sponger who, like a pernicious bacillus, spreads over wider and wider areas according as some favorable area attracts him....He poisons the blood of others...."[10] Following Luther and other philosophers of Aryan superiority, Hitler believed in a worldwide Jewish conspiracy and that Jews were vermin and lice. This portrayal was repeated in Nazi propaganda throughout the period of the mass murder. Many firsthand accounts have been preserved. A Jewish smuggler, for example, who escaped from the Warsaw Ghetto, provides the following description: "When I was in Aryan Warsaw, I sometimes tried, in spite of the danger, to tear down the large posters showing a hideous Jew with a louse-ridden beard. 'Jew-louse-typhoid,' it said. We were germ carriers, vermin."[11] These myths and the accompanying propaganda effectively functioned to dehumanize the potential victims and justify their extermination. It is legitimate to kill vermin. In essence, this was the key to the creation of a target population for which extermination was justifiable.

The Aryan mythology is not the only example of cultural myth functioning to dehumanize potential victims. All racist terminology is part of such mythology. In cases such as these, language becomes a powerful cutural weapon as it portrays entire groups of pc ople as not quite human. Other examples involve the use of color symbolism, which forms a powerful set of negative stereotypes and images, with black as negative and evil, white as positive and beautiful. This type of racist terminology takes on other less implicit forms. During the Vietnam War, negative symbolism was used to dehumanize the Vietnamese people, characterizing them as *gooks*, *dinks*, and *slant-eyes*.[12] In an earlier period of American history, native Americans were negatively labeled to prepare for their eventual destruction. They were saddled with terms such as *Indian*, *savage*, *infidel*, *heathen*, and *barbarian*.[13] A prime example of this dehumanizing symbolism can be found in the description by one Alexander Whitaker, a minister in Henrico, Virginia, who wrote in 1613:

> ...let the miserable condition of these naked slaves of the divell move you to compassion....Wherefore they serve the divell for fear, after a most base manner, sacrificing sometimes (as I have heard) their own children to him....Their priests....are no other but such as our English witches are. They live naked in bodie, as if their shame of their sins deserved no covering: Their names are as naked as their bodie: They esteem it a virtue to lie, deceive and steal as their master the divell teacheth to them.[14]

How guilt-free were the atrocities that resulted from this process of dehumanization? As one United States soldier put it when discussing his having killed an old woman in Vietnam, "the gun just went off by itself. You know it really bothers me...I mean the thing that bothers me about killing her is that it doesn't bother me."[15] I could amplify this point with numerous additional examples. Even this brief explication, however, should clearly show the relationship between dehumanizing symbols and the cultural conditions for guilt-free massacre.

The cultural myths that dehumanize the potential victims develop over time and may be embedded in a culture. They even may become part of the culture's conventional wisdom and be transmitted unconsciously through common expressions. Consider the phrase, "to Jew someone down," used as a synonym for cheating a person out of money. These dehumanizing stereotypes eventually find their way into the psyches of individual members of a culture. Consequently, a close relationship exists between cultural conditions and psychological conditions of guilt-free massacre.

Psychological Conditions

The psychological conditions for guilt-free massacre focus directly on the possibility that, given the right circumstances, any individual might be placed in a position in which his or her morality, or sense of right and wrong, is compromised. The basic psychological condition for guilt-free massacre involves unquestioning obedience to authority.[16] Following orders takes precedence over all other considerations. Under these conditions, an individual no longer feels responsible for his or her actions. Individuals can define themselves as instruments for carrying out the wishes of others. The classic example, of course, is Adolf Eichmann.

Eichmann never felt guilt. His attitude toward his indictment, revealed indirectly as recounted by Hannah Arendt, was that it was wrong: "With the killing of the Jews I had nothing to do. I never killed a Jew or a non–Jew, for that matter—I never killed any human being. I never gave an order to kill either a Jew or a non–Jew; I just did not do it."[17] Yet Eichmann left little doubt that if he had received an order to kill, he would have done so. In fact, Eichmann recalled that he would have had a "bad conscience only if he had not done what he had been ordered to do—to ship millions of men, women, and children to their death with great zeal and the most meticulous care."[18] Eichmann, consequently, has become the prototype of the person whose sense of individual morality has been reoriented from the general Judeo–Christian concepts. He felt shame or pride not in the fact that he engineered the extermination of millions of people, but in how efficient he was in carrying out the orders given to him, or those he thought would be given to him, by persons who occupied positions above him in the hierarchy of authority. Still, Eichmann is not the only manifestation of this bureaucratic ethic.

The depressing example of Franz Stangl is equally revealing. As commandant of the Sobibor and Treblinka extermination camps, he was one of only a few individuals to hold such an infamous position of authority. Of them, only Stangl and Rudolf Hess were brought to trial; they were also the only ones to leave an extensive written reflection on what they had done.[19] From these interviews, Stangl emerges as a person unable or unwilling "to make responsible decisions to make the fundamental choice between right and wrong."[20] In fact, during several stages of his infamous career, Stangl had the opportunity to choose whether to proceed along the path of becoming a destroyer of life or whether to abandon his ambition for success in the Nazi hierarchy and function as a lesser bureaucrat. In each case he behaved as a typical member of his culture. He followed orders without question, he did his job, he abdicated his responsibility to make a moral choice between defense of life and administration of death. Like Eichmann, Hess, and others, he chose to become an administrator of death, and he carried out his task with disturbing efficiency.

Efficiency in carrying out orders was highly valued by the bureaucratic hierarchy. It may, in fact, remain highly prized in contemporary society. "Old–fashioned" ideas of morality and responsibility may be in the process of being replaced, so that, as Milgram argues, the morals of contemporary society begin to take on a different shape. We should consider whether morality may be defined today, as it was for Eichmann and Stangl, as how well a person carries out assigned tasks, no matter what a task may entail.

This is an extremely important aspect of the psychological condition for guilt–free massacre, because it emphasizes the possibility that acts of human destructiveness are not necessarily committed by noticeably psychopathic deranged monsters. Rather, what has come to be referred to as the "banality of evil"[21] stresses that such acts are most likely committed by ordinary people. As one observer has pointed out, however difficult it may be, we must begin to understand that many of the great monsters of history, such as Eichmann and Stangl, were not unusual examples of their culture. Heinrich Himmler, for example, has been characterized as "pedestrian, unimaginative—in a word ordinary."[22] In addition, we are now aware that German citizens were attracted to Hitler on a rather large scale, and they supported, or at least did not oppose, the anti–Semitic platform of the Nazis. Even the mobile killing units that roamed Soviet territory were composed of "normal" people. Lawyers, philosophers, teachers, workers, religious people—all took part in the destruction of the European Jews.[23]

These controversial ideas force us to focus on our own vulnerability and to question the circumstances of obedience. Difficult personal questions necessarily arise. Where does one draw the line in obeying authority? Should a person follow all orders, even if the ultimate result is inhumane or evil? Such ideas about obedience are closely tied to the third prerequisite for guilt–free massacre—the political conditions.

Political Conditions

The transition from the cultural and psychological conditions for mass murder to its becoming a reality occurs through political socialization.[24] How people view a political system is intimately tied to how it is organized and presented as they are growing up. As children we are exposed to the cultural–political myths and legends common to our environment, and these act as foundations for our adult opinions and behaviors. These opinions and behavioral predispositions are transmitted to our psyches through the process of political socialization.

The process operates simply. Born into an already operative political culture, a young person receives the norms of that culture from accepted agents of socialization. The young person, in turn, accepts or rejects the norms and acts accordingly. The content of what is transmitted and learned may vary from culture to culture, though some norms find their way to most people.

Of course, there are always exceptions and variations. The child born and raised in a black or Mexican American community probably does not learn to view the police the same way a child born into a white middle–class culture does. These variations mean that the process is complex. They also emphasize the importance of culture in determining the boundaries of the process.

These boundaries are taught to every person in an attempt to make them fit the existing definition of what a person is and how a person should act. These boundaries include political and cultural definitions of deviance. They are mechanisms through which existing norms are internalized. As summed up by one very perceptive observer, "The first twenty years of the young person's life are spent functioning as a subordinate element in an authority system....The net result of this experience is the internalization of the social order—that is the set of axioms by which social life is conducted. And the chief axiom is: do what the man in charge says."[25] This is important, because the most efficient means of inducing obedience is to implant in people through political socialization existing definitions of accepted behavior. If people are convinced that these definitions are legitimate and if they become internalized, then those in power need not resort to force to put down dissident elements (those who exceed the defined boundaries). Obviously, if we all internalize the accepted definitions and obey, there will be no dissidents.

If a nation contains cultural strands emphasizing rigidity and obedience and these are internalized through socialization, then these cultural imperatives stressing obedience may become preconditons for participation in mass murder. Consider, in particular, how people learn to view authority. When individuals begin to identify strongly with authority, when they look outside themselves for solutions to personal or political problems, they are also less likely to believe in themselves and have a strong sense of self-esteem. This leads to a personality less likely to engage in political activity questioning the existing system. If I believe in my own incapacity, I then look for leaders, for someone to tell me what to do and what to believe and how to behave. The impact of this has been pointed out by Milgram, who surmises that our identity as individuals possibly is defined by how we relate to or identify with authority. Individual identity thus becomes intertwined with the state and its leaders, and they are used as reference points for self-definition.

By implication, we internalize artifically constructed mythologies and make them part of our psyches. They become part of our world view and may or may not be reinforced by cues from political and social leaders.

One mechanism for reinforcing deference to authority involves rituals of induction. All organizations socialize new members. Not only cultures and nation states, but social, cultural, and political organizations as well. The Unites States Congress and state legislatures, for example, conduct classes for new members in a process similar to medieval apprenticeship.[26] More overt examples may be found in military organizations and in the Nazi SS. Philip Caputo sums up military indoctrination as follows:

...By the third week, we had learned to obey orders instantly and in unison, without thinking....

The mental and physical abuse has several objectives. They were calculated first to eliminate the weak who were collectively known as "unsats," for unsatisfactory. The reasoning was that anyone who could not take being shouted at and kicked in the ass once in awhile could never withstand the rigors of combat. But such abuse was also designed to destroy each man's sense of self-worth, to make him feel worthless until he proved himself equal to the Corp's exacting standards.[27]

Once the self-worth was destroyed, what message replaced it? Caputo continues:

Throughout, we were subjected to intense indoctrination, which seemed to borrow from Communist brain-washing techniques. We had to chant slogans while running: "Hut-two-three-four, I love the Marine Corps." And before meals: "Sir, the United States Marines; since 1775, the most invincible fighting force in the history of man. Gung ho! Gung ho! Pray for war!" Like the slogans of revolutionaries, these look ludicrous in print, but when recited in unison by a hundred voices, they have a weird hypnotic effect on a man. The psychology of the mob, of the *Bund* rally, takes command of his will and he finds himself shouting that nonsense even though he knows it is nonsense. In time, he begins to believe that he really does love the Marine Corps, that it is invincible, and that there is nothing improper in praying for war, the event in which the Corps periodically has justified its existence and achieved its apotheosis.[28]

The result, of course, is obedience. One is not supposed to consider the consequences of the acts one is ordered to undertake. When the orders are consistently reinforced by high ranking officials, those who have been trained to do so follow them.

William Calley thought he received a consistent message, "eliminate them,"[29] that is, eliminate the people of My Lai. Or as Lifton confirms, borrowing the words of a My Lai survivor, "'It's okay to kill them,' and in fact 'that's what you're supposed to do'—or as a former marine received it: 'You've gotta go to Vietnam, you've gotta kill the gooks.'"[30] A similar process is revealed in the examples of Treblinka and Sobibor. Franz Stangl, summing up his early training for the Austrian police force, says the "training was tough. They called it the 'Vienna School'....They were a sadistic lot. They drilled the feeling into us that everyone was against us: that all men were rotten."[31]

The most unambiguous case, perhaps, of blind obedience result-ing from ritual induction may be seen in the Nazi SS. First the SS candidate had to prove his Aryan pedigree. After doing so and expe-riencing training of the most dehumanizing type, the SS candidate was allowed to swear the Kith and Kin oath:

I swear to thee, Adolf Hitler,

As Fuhrer and Chancellor of the German Reich,

Loyalty and Bravery.

I vow to thee and to the superiors whom thou shall appoint

Obedience unto death.

So help me God.[32]

Afterwards, the candidate memorized the SS catechism, which con-sisted of a series of questions and answers such as the following:

Q: Why do we believe in Germany and the Fuhrer?

A: Because we believe in God, we believe in Germany which He created in His world and in the Fuhrer Adolf Hitler, whom He has sent us.[33]

This was followed by a regimen of rigorous discipline and control designed to produce men whose obedience was unquestioning. In one of his more impassioned moments, Hitler said, "And if I tell my SS troops that they must fight tanks with walking sticks, they will run out and do what they are told!"[34]

Obedience is justified in the name of God, the Fuhrer, the state, or some mission. Cues that reinforce obedience are sent by people occupying important social, cultural, or political positions. If the na-tional mythology emphasizes obedience, leaders can easily manipu-late it to convince potential participants that mass murder is justified. Hence, if people in high positions engage in dehumanizing symboliza-tions of ethnic or religious groups, they send a message that it is justi-fied to discriminate or act in some other, perhaps more serious, nega-tive fashion against a particular group. Leaders who engage in dehu-manizing symbolism or talk of violent action as necessary in defense of a state or a way or life may well be preparing for the victimization of the people who will become the targets of their rhetoric.

An ever-ready supply of people is willing to act out hostile im-pulses reinforced by those in positions of influence. Stangl refers to just such an incident when he points out that he was profoundly af-fected in his early days by Cardinal Innitzer's call to Catholics to "co-operate" with the Nazis, as well as by the fact that many political leaders capitulated "at once" to the Nazis.[35]

Leaders prepare a population for genocide by positing a connec-tion between the well-being of a particular country or group and obe-dience to the leaders. This results in the view that the leaders must be correct simply because they are leaders. Again, by way of illustration, William Calley comments about his situation:

I was a run–of–the–mill average guy: I still am, I always said, *The people in Washington are smarter than me.* If intelligent people told me, "Communism's bad. It's going to engulf us. To take us in," I believe them. I had to. I was sure it could happen: the Russians could come in a parachute drop. Or a HALO drop or some submarines or space capsules even.[36]

Investing leaders with this aura of invincibility and authority further results in a situation where those who carry out the orders are absolved of responsibility. Acting on the basis of orders given by higher authority and for a higher good—the nation state, God, whatever—they see themselves as agents of the state or of divine will. Actions are not then individual actions for which a person must take responsibility. These acts are seen as organizational behavior. If, as Milgram argues, morality is redefined in the organizational context as how efficiently one carries out orders, the orders and the actions are not seriously questioned. In addition, participation in this organizational context provides a sense of identity that may have been precarious or obliterated by a harsh life or by the chaos of a particular historical crisis. Such provisions of identity are evident in the autobiographical statements of early Nazis detailed in Peter Merkl's *The Making of a Stormtrooper*:

When a stormtrooper put on his uniform and went to do his "service" he literally stripped off his humdrum worker's life, or meek bourgeois habit, and became a heroic superman to himself and his comrades. Marching and fighting in closed formation, in particular, he felt powerful and masculine beyond compare. Longing for the heroics of World War I and for the machismo of the all–male cult of the veterans or Youth Movement group, to him the "fighting years were the best time of our lives."[37]

The political conditions for the commission of guilt–free massacre are complicated and closely related to the psychological and cultural conditions. Basically, the cultural myths are reinforced and transmitted through political socialization. Mass murder is committed in the name of some higher good. Leaders do not intend for their troops or the people they lead to commit acts of evil, and when they do, the acts are not defined as evil. Acts of guilt–free massacre are justified and responsibility is diffused. The political conditions interact with the cultural and psychological conditions to allow murder without guilt.

Why People Kill

The circumstances under which guilt–free massacre may occur may begin with cultural conditions, which involve the development of cultural and racial myths and stereotypes. Actually, the cultural conditions, in many ways, are responsible for selecting the eventual target, as the cultural myths point the way to identifying the most likely victims for extermination. A second factor, the psychological conditions, requires obedience to authority by individuals, the people, who will pull the triggers and carry out the orders. The political conditions combine the giving of orders and justification for the acts of destruction. In addition, the transmission of the cultural and psychological imperatives interact with political conditions, since the process of political socialization involves inculcating both cultural and psychological rationalizations. Ultimately, if we view mass murder as being carried out, at least in part, in response to these conditions, we are left with the profoundly disturbing conclusion that acts of large–scale destruction of human life might be committed by any individual or nation under the right cultural, psychological, or political circumstances.

Understanding the conditions that promote guilt–free massacre does not necessarily mean these acts will not occur again. Yet, we must understand the past and incorporate, as an integral part of our learning experience, information about genocide and guilt–free massacre so that we may attempt to avoid the depressing fate of Rudolf Hess. Sitting in his Nuremberg cell, Hess summed up his life by noting that he felt he could have done nothing different: "I had nothing to say; I could only say 'Jawohl!' We could only execute orders without thinking about it....from our entire training the thought of refusing an order just didn't enter one's head, regardless of what kind of order it was."[38]

Acknowledgments

Anyone foolish enough to attempt to add to the literature concerned with mass murder and genocide must add a necessary disclaimer. The material included in this essay is borrowed, perhaps stolen, from several thinkers who have profoundly influenced my views of human destructiveness. They follow, with mention of their significant works, in alphabetical order: Hannah Arendt, *Eichmann in Jerusalem: A Report on the Banality of Evil*; Terrence Des Pres, *The Survivor: An Anatomy of Life in the Death Camps*; Erich Fromm, *The Anatomy of Human Destructiveness*; Helen Fein, *Accounting for Genocide*; Raul Hilberg, *The Destruction of the European Jews*; Irving Louis Horowitz, *Taking Lives: Genocide and State Power*; Robert Jay Lifton, *Home from the War*; Stanley Milgram, *Obedience to Authority*; Barrington Moore, Jr., *Injustice: The Social Bases of Obedience and Revolt*; Richard L. Rubenstein, *The Cunning of History*; Nevitt Sanford and Craig Comstock, eds., *Sanctions for Evil*.

Two recent works attempt a comprehensive theory of genocide. They are Israel W. Charny, *How Can We Commit the Unthinkable*, and Leo Kuper, *Genocide*.

This work is consequently derivative, though I hope not trivial.

Notes

1. Elie Wiesel, *One Generation After* (New York: Pocket Books, 1965), p. 15.

2. Theodore Adorno maintained that after Auschwitz poetry could no longer flourish because silence was the only appropriate response, as discussed by George Steiner in *Language and Silence* (New York: Atheneum, 1977), p. 53. For a vivid analysis of high culture and barbarism, see George Steiner, *In Bluebeard's Castle: Some Notes toward a Definition of Culture* (New Haven: Yale University Press, 1971). The novelist William Styron has written that "Auschwitz itself remains inexplicable" and that a writer can only give testimony to the effect that "absolute evil is never extinguished from the world," from *Sophie's Choice* (New York: Random House, 1976), p. 513. For an elaboration of Styron's ideas, see his introduction to Richard L. Rubenstein, *The Cunning of History: The Holocaust and the American Future* (New York: Harper and Row, 1978), pp. vii–xiv.

3. See Robert Jay Lifton, *Home from the War* (New York: Simon and Schuster, 1973), p. 127.

4. Troy Duster, "Conditions for Guilt-Free Massacre," in Nevitt Sanford and Craig Comstock, eds., *Sanctions for Evil* (Boston: Beacon Press, 1971), pp. 25–36. Duster actually distinguishes three forms of guilt: "the commission of an act regarded as reprehensible, immoral, illegal or the like, the subjective feeling state of actors,... [and] the pronouncement of culpability by men formally empowered to make such pronouncements" (p. 26).

5. Ibid, pp. 25–36. Duster identifies six conditions: (1) the denial of the victims' humanity, (2) subordination of the individual to organizations, (3) connection between individual responsibility and rules of organization, (4) secrecy and isolation, (5) existence of a target population, and (6) developing the "motivation to conduct a massacre."

6. The relationship between racial myths, culture, and oppression is explored in Leon Poliakov, *The Aryan Myth: A History of Racist and Nationalist Ideas in Europe* (New York: New American Library, 1971); and George L. Mosse, *Toward the Final Solution: A History of European Racism* (New York: Harper and Row, 1978). The connection between culture and genocide or oppression is examined in Marvin Harris, *Cows, Pigs, Wars and Witches: The Riddles of Culture* (New York: Vintage Books, 1973); Jules Henry, *Culture Against Man* (New York: Vintage Books, 1965); and Ernest Becker, *Escape from Evil* (New York: The Free Press, 1975). On the connection between religion and repression, see Jules Isaac, *The Teaching of Contempt: Christian Roots of Anti-Semitism*, trans. Helen Weaver (New York: Holt, Rinehart and Winston, 1964).

7. Raul Hiberg, *The Destruction of the European Jews* (New York: Harper and Row, 1961). Also see Lucy S. Dawidowicz, *The War Against the Jews* (New York: Bantam Books, 1975); and Mosse, *Toward the Final Solution*.

8. Martin Luther, *On the Jews and Their Lies*, cited in Hilberg, *Destruction of the European Jews*, p. 9.

9. Ibid., p. 10.

10. Hitler, cited in Hilberg.

11. Martin Gray, *For Those I Loved* (Boston: Little, Brown and Company, 1971), p. 82.

12. See Lifton, *Home from the War*. This phenomenon is captured powerfully in many firsthand accounts, such as Philip Caputo, *A Rumor of War* (New York: Ballantine Books, 1977); Michael Herr, *Dispatches* (New York: Avon Books, 1978); and Seymour M. Hersh, *My Lai 4: A Report on the Massacre and Its Aftermath* (New York: Vintage Books, 1970).

13. Robert F. Berkhoffer, Jr., *The White Man's Indian* (New York: Vintage Books, 1979).

14. Ibid., p. 19.

15. Caputo, *A Rumor of War*, p. 297.

16. The most perceptive discussion of obedience remains Stanley Milgram, *Obedience to Authority* (New York: Harper and Row, 1974). Also instructive are the discussions in Richard Sennett, *Authority* (New York: Alfred A. Knopf, 1980); and Barrington Moore, Jr., *Injustice: The Social Bases of Obedience and Revolt* (White Plains, N.Y.: M.E. Sharpe, Inc., 1978).

17. Hannah Arendt, *Eichmann in Jerusalem: A Report on the Banality of Evil* (New York: Penguin Books, 1963), p. 221.

18. Ibid., p. 25.

19. Gitta Sereny, *Into That Darkness* (New York: Vintage Books, 1974). And, of course, Rudolf Hess is reputed to have stated, "I am completely normal. Even while I was carrying out the task of extermination I led a normal family life and so on," in "Rudolph Hess—The Man from the Crowd," in Joachim C. Fest, *The Face of the Third Reich* (New York: Pantheon Books, 1970), pp. 276–287.

20. Sereny, *Into That Darkness*, p. 367.

21. Arendt, *Eichmann in Jerusalem*; also by Arendt, "Organized Guilt and Universal Responsibility," in Roger W. Smith, ed., *Guilt: Man and Society* (Garden City, N.Y.: Anchor Books, 1971), pp. 255–267.

22. G.S. Garber, *History of the SS* (New York: David McKay, 1978), p. 211.

23. Hilberg, *Destruction of the European Jews*, pp. 177–256.

24. Since 1959, when Hyman published his pioneering study of political socialization, political scientists have been busy attempting to understand how the process operates and what it eventually results in

when the child becomes an adult. The derivative systems theory studies of Easton and Dennis, through the "benevolent leader" studies of Greenstein and even down to their contemporary extensions, have focused on the maintenance of stability and perceptions of political authority. After years of important critical interpretations, the focus on stability and benevolence, and a tendency to dismiss cultural variations, remains a major thrust of the studies. See Herbert Hyman, *Political Socialization* (New York: The Free Press, 1959); David Easton and Jack Dennis, *Children in the Political System* (New York: McGraw–Hill, 1969); Fred I. Greenstein, *Children and Politics*, (New York: Yale University Press, 1965); also by Greenstein, "The Benevolent Leader: Children's Images of Political Authority," *American Political Science Review* 54 (December 1960): 934–943; and "The Benevolent Leader Revisited: Children's Images of Political Leaders in Three Democracies," *American Political Science Review* 69 (December 1975): 1,371–1,398. Dissenting interpretations include Dean Jaros, Herbert Hirsch, and Frederick J. Fleron, Jr., "The Malevolent Leader: Political Socialization in an American Sub-Culture," *American Political Science Review* 62 (June 1968): 564–575; Herbert Hirsch, *Poverty and Politicization: Political Socialization in an American Sub-Culture* (New York: The Free Press, 1971); and Herbert Hirsch and Armando Gutierrez, *Learning to be Militant: Ethnic Identity and the Development of Political Militance in a Chicano Community* (San Francisco: R & E Research Associates, 1977).

25. Milgram, *Obedience to Authority*, pp. 137–138.

26. Herbert Hirsch, "The Political Socialization of State Legislators: A Re-Examination," in Herbert Hirsch and M. Donald Hancock, eds., *Comparative Legislative Systems: A Reader in Theory and Research* (New York: The Free Press, 1971), pp. 98–106. The classic study, of course, is Donald R. Matthews, *U.S. Senators and Their World* (New York: Vintage, 1960). On some other socialization experiences, see William A. Lucas, "Anticipatory Socialization and the ROTC," in Charles C. Moskos, Jr., ed., *Public Opinion and the Military Establishment* (Beverly Hills: Sage, 1971), pp. 99–134; and Stanton Wheeler, "The Structure of Formerly Organized Socialization Settings," in Orville Brim and Stanton Wheeler, *Socialization after Childhood* (New York: John Wiley, 1966), pp. 53–116.

27. Caputo, *A Rumor of War*, pp. 9–10.

28. Ibid., p. 12.

29. William L. Calley, "Lieutenant Calley: His Own Story," in Jay W. Baird, ed., *From Nuremberg to My Lai* (Lexington, Mass.: D.C. Heath, 1972), p. 222.

30. From Vietnam Veterans Against the War, *The Winter Soldier Investigation: An Inquiry into American War Crimes* (Boston: Beacon Press, 1972), p. 5, cited in Lifton, *Home from the War*, pp. 42–43.

31. Sereny, *Into That Darkness*, p. 28.

32. Graber, *History of the SS*, p. 28.

33. Ibid., p. 83.

34. Ibid., pp. 89–90.

35. Sereny, *Into That Darkness*, p. 30.

36. Calley, "His Own Story," p. 225. The tone of Calley's deference is further amplified when he states, "Now, I hate to say it, but most people know a lot more about communism than I do. In school, I never thought about it. I just dismissed it. I looked at communism as a Southerner looks at the Negro, supposedly. *It's evil. It's bad*" (p. 224).

37. Peter H. Merkl, *The Making of a Stormtrooper* (Princeton: The University Press, 1980), p. 231.

38. "Rudolf Hess," in Fest, *Face of the Third Reich*, p. 280.

III

Cultural Manifestations of Anti-Semitism

While overt anti-Semitism has been manifested to a lesser extent in the United States than in Europe, the United States has not been totally free of its poison. The ancient roots outlined by Rubenstein have had modern consequences, as outlined by Hirsch, and the immigrants to the United States brought with them accompanying traditions and anti-Semitic mythologies learned in their native environments. Thus, European anti-Semitism was transplanted to American soil where it grew into a different sort of plant.

In the early period of American history, Jews were rather insignificant in number, and anti-Semitism was not nearly as common or virulent as in Europe. The social structure in America was more fluid. Jews were rarely used as scapegoats here. Social prejudice against Jews did appear in the 1870s with the rise of German Jews to economic affluence. It was manifested among rich Gentiles, who attempted to maintain exclusivity in hotels, clubs, and universities.

Analysts therefore hypothesized that American anti-Semitism is related closely to economics or class. In fact, as Dobkowski points out in "A Historical Survey of Anti-Semitism in America Prior to World War II," American anti-Semitism has been seen primarily as economic, that is, related to a downturn in the economy or to the economic visibility of Jews. The problem with the economic interpretation, as Dobkowski also points out, is that by focusing on overt manifestations expressed as class resentment, it overlooks the presence of other significant sources of anti-Semitic beliefs (the ideological, the historical, and the cultural) and consequently may underestimate the volume and intensity of prejudice. Certainly anti-Semitism has economic roots, but it also has ideological roots and, one hastens to add, cultural and psychological ones as well.

Dobkowski begins by asking, "Has America been different?" Even in America, where anti-Semitism has been less violent and overt than in Europe, Dobkowski emphasizes (quoting Emil Fackenheim), "'America too has exacted its price. To be sure, the price seemed a just price—that of becoming American—which all had equally to pay. Yet some were more equal than others, and the fact that this inequality remained ideologically disguised' was to have serious consequences."

European study of anti-Semitism placed it as a central indicator, Dobkowski tells us, of the "basic health of any society." American scholars, however, have shown a relative neglect of anti-Semitism, tending, as Dobkowski argues, "to view anti-Semitism as an exception, a quirk of fate, an abnormal situation caused by temporary social and economic factors." This relative neglect has resulted in de-emphasizing "the importance of literary and social stereotyping as indices of prejudice," leaving the ideological aspects of this prejudice unexamined. According to Dobkowski, "this ideological assault...nurtured a particularly unfavorable public perception of Jews that is still reflected in American public opinion."

Only in the 1920s "did American scholars begin to recognize the existence of anti-Semitism as a significant development in American history." Further motivated by the Holocaust, American scholars, Dobkowski observes, have become more attuned to investigating and attempting to "understand the social, economic, religious, and psychological factors that predispose some individuals and societies to reactions of extreme hostility and hatred directed towards racial and religious groups."

A large amount of this scholarly effort was concentrated on studies of public opinion or attitudes toward Jews. The survey research, which has recorded a decrease in anti-Semitic beliefs over the years, suffers from one glaring weakness—it fails to explain the earlier historic manifestations of anti-Semitism. To remedy this, Dobkowski points out that scholars have created several different frameworks as explanatory theories. Marxist economic analysis, used in the 1940s, gave way in the 1950s to what has come to be called the generation of "consensus historians." Not until the late 1960s did American historians become "more sensitive to the issue of American anti-Semitism and the role of ideology."

Of course, this is part of a larger trend of revisionist history that involved a "critical rethinking of assumptions long taken for granted concerning the political, economic, and social reality of our past." This revisionism was tied as well to a renewed interest in Jewish history and, particularly, a "growing interest in the Holocaust," which was "spurred on by the 1962 Eichmann trial, the 1967 Arab-Israeli war...and the emergence of Eli Wiesel as folk hero and witness to atrocity." In addition, "revelations of...American apathy, if not complicity, in the tragedy of the Holocaust" sparked further interest in anti-Semitism. Dobkowski proceeds to analyze, as part of this intellectual tradition, the image of the Jew in the United States. The negative images have been present from the early days of Christianity and were, as Dobkowski argues, "staples of newspaper and magazine articles, plays, the dime novels,...perpetrated by both the famous and unknown of the American literary scene." Even in America, the Jew was depersonalized, stereotyped, and ultimately dehumanized.

Despite all this, Dobkowski notes, American anti-Semitism was less violent than its European relatives. Though "America never visited mass physical oppression upon its Jews," many "subtle types of oppression—economic, social, and cultural—" were "also damaging and painful." Dobkowski concludes that while "America may have been different, it was not different enough."

The images and stereotypes perceptively cited by Dobkowski as the fundmental building blocks of anti-Semitic attitudes are analyzed in greater detail in Chapters 5 and 6, which present examples of anti-Semitism in American and English literature. Images and stereotypes may become an accepted part of a culture as a result of their treatment in and transmission through literature. In the United States, Kessner writes in "More Devils Than Hell Can Hold: Anti-Semitism in American Literature," anti-Semitism appealed largely to the mythic image of Jews as "the devil's agents on earth." This image is commonly associated with "one eponymous Jew named Judas."

...The same archetypal figures occur over and over again. Only of that time or this place they wear different dress.

This explains the persistence of a fundamental mythic image, stereotype if you will, of the Jew in English literature and, at a certain historical point, in its descendent, American literature. The essentially demonic, evil, mythic projection of the Jew appears in literature from the New Testament characterization of Judas, the betrayer for money, on down to our own times, though that projection is given a local habitation and a name.

The latest form of expressing the "Jew animus" is its geopolitical version—Zionism. Kessner traces the image of devil's agent from its earliest to its most recent manifestation in American literature, with the Zionist as the latest agent in history. The reader may be surprised by the names of some of the authors whose writings contain anti-Semitic elements.

According to the last essay in this section, Sharp's "Shakespeare's Shylock and Ours," the vilifying portrayal of the Jew as devil's agent is clearly drawn in Shakespeare's *The Merchant of Venice*: "...Shylock was a villian, a wicked and wrongheaded man whose Jewish identity and faith were portrayed as contributing to his unjust and cruel intents." Yet Shakespeare, although a product of his environment, apparently was unique in presenting an image of the Jew not only as mythically diabolical but also as a human being. Sharp believes that Shakespeare created a "Jewish villain who yet retains the essential dignity of his humanity," and this different perception was "nothing short of wonderful, especially in a play created for a mass audience composed almost exclusively of rabid anti-Semites."

Elizabethan literature was filled with images of the Jew as the devil's agent. Shakespeare's depiction fits the stereotypical image, yet transcends it, especially in the "Hath not a Jew eyes?" speech. Sharp asserts that Shakespeare, trapped by the prejudices of his time, also attempted to communicate the "recognition that Jews, too, have the same human rights as Christians." The existence of expressions such as this allows us to conclude with two hopeful accounts in the final section, which nonetheless should not be taken as naive delusions that anti-Semitism has disappeared.

Chapter 4

A Historical Survey of Anti-Semitism in America Prior to World War II

Michael N. Dobkowski

Has America been different? This question, as theologian Emil Fackenheim has noted, became central in the Jewish mind ever since a once-civilized European country exploded in this century in an unprecedented orgy of anti-Semitism and genocide. It is a question that permits no easy answers. "On the one hand, the land of immigrants offered Jews a home on terms more equal than tradition-bound Europe; unencumbered by medieval traditions, it was largely unencumbered by medieval" and Christian-inspired anti-Semitism as well. "On the other hand, America too has exacted its price. To be sure, the price seemed a just price—that of becoming American—which all had equally to pay. Yet some were more equal than others, and the fact that this inequality remained ideologically disguised" was to have serious consequences.[1]

To be sure, a difference exists between Europe and America. After the emancipation of the Jews, Fackenheim indicates, the French and German peoples "typically expected Jews to outdo themselves in gratitude for ceasing to be persecuted." In contrast, "America expected Jews merely to privatize whatever part of their religio-cultural heritage they wished to preserve," while presuming everyone would count equally in the civic culture.[2] "No wonder...Jewish immigrants responded enthusiastically to both the expectation and the promise, and to the extent to which the promise and the expectation were and could be realities Jewish emancipation in America has been a success." However, it was an emancipation (perhaps inevitably) limited by ideology. Did the separation of church and state completely destroy Christian imperialism? "Had the New World rid itself entirely of the anti-Semitism of the old? It is surely not only the American idea but also a well-founded fear of...prejudice," heightened by events in this century, that made "American Jews demand to be treated simply as Americans....Surely this fear together with the knowledge that Jewishness is not and cannot be either purely private or purely religious gives rise to the tension" between cultural integration and ethnic survival.[3]

Given this reality, the relative neglect of anti-Semitism by students of American history contrasts interestingly with the intense fascination it has held for scholars of European history. The latter assigned to anti-Semitism an extraordinary importance arguing that critical attitudes towards Jews indicate the basic health of any society. "Anti-Semitism, in this view, is not just a serious problem in human relations; it is the very archetype of prejudice."[4] To paraphrase Dostoyevsky, European historians maintained that a civilization can be judged by how it treats Jews and other vulnerable groups. The study of anti-Semitism for these scholars must be understood not just as parochial concern, but rather as the study of the essence of the culture itself.

Thus historians of European Jewry like Jacob Katz, Shmuel Ettinger, Yehuda Bauer, and Leon Poliakov have made anti-Semitism one of their central themes as they emphasize the pogroms, expulsions, discrimination, and annihilation. This has been true especially for many post-Holocaust historians for whom the murder of six million Jews was the logical culmination of the social, economic, intellectual, and religious currents dominant in Europe during the past 1,800 years.[5]

Historians of American Jewry, in contrast, have tended to view anti-Semitism as an exception, a quirk of fate, an abnormal situation caused by temporary social and economic factors. As John Higham has pointed out, no political, economic, or social movement, no religious development, no deep social crisis (with the possible exception of the Populist movement) has been associated with anti-Semitism.[6] Accordingly, historians have rarely taken more than a passing interest in studying it. In keeping with this neglect, when scholars have examined the phenomenon, they have played down, for the most part, the importance of literary and social stereotyping as indices of prejudice.[7] This is unfortunate, for "conceivably, ideology drove a wedge between Jews and Gentiles simply by sharpening negative stereotypes."[8] Minds were often made up before any personal encounter with Jews could transpire.[9] This ideological conflict, pervasive in American society, nurtured a particularly unfavorable public perception of Jews that is still reflected in American public opinion and that negatively affected its victims. The conflict of ideologies also may have contributed to the internalization of stereotypes resulting in self-hatred and the drive towards assimilation. Scholarly literature is scattered and inchoate, focusing on the more tangible aspects of anti-Semitism and prejudice, rather than the ideological and psychological consequences of decades of stereotyping and the pressures to assimilate (in Europe there was the stick, in America the carrot). We therefore lack a systematic understanding of the factors that have divided Jew and Christian in America. Another problem involves the degree of uncertainty and theoretical fuzziness surrounding the nature of anti-Semitism.

Ultimately, we are left with studies that do not define anti–Semitism. Nor do they create working typologies of anti–Semitism, something Ben Halpern has successfully attempted.[10]

Notwithstanding the tendency of many to see anti–Semitism behind every furtive glance and frustrated desire (the "I knows it when I sees it" attitude), clearly not every negative statement or sentiment regarding Jews is anti–Semitic. To some extent, Jewish immigrants to America experienced hostility simply for being impoverished, unacculturated foreigners.[11] American pride in this country as a haven for the oppressed and the liberal traditions of tolerance, individuality, and equal opportunity helped create, as Jonathan Sarna has pointed out, the ambivalent attitudes Americans have had concerning Jews, often combining feelings of hostility with feelings of friendship and acceptance.[12] Moreover, mitigating circumstances contributed toward tolerance within the historical tradition of American Christianity. John Higham has argued, for example, that a certain strain of sentiment among American Protestants admired Jews and Judaism. Puritan orthodoxy held that the Jews were God's chosen people, miraculously saved and sustained as proof of God's greatness, a view that lent itself to sympathy and positive identification with the Jews.[13]

Not until the 1920s did American scholars—prodded by the nativism of the preceding decades, Henry Ford's Dearborn *Independent* anti–Semitic propaganda campaign, and the fulminations of quasifascist groups—begin to recognize the existence of anti–Semitism as a significant development in American history.[14] Walter Lippmann, Frank Boas, Robert E. Park, and Horace Kallen studied racial prejudice and ethnocentricity in the United States in response to the racial and ethnic xenophobia that overcame American society during and following World War I.[15] Their perspectives, based on a faith in cultural relativism, were joined a decade later to the theories of social psychologists Gardiner Murphy and Richard Crutchfield, who responded to the demagogic madness of the 1930s by identifying anti–Semitism with the attitudes of groups who supported fascism, imperialism, economic conservatism, and isolation.[16]

After the Holocaust, American scholars returned to the question of anti–Semitism. Prominent social scientists and psychologists attempted to analyze and understand these social, economic, religious, and psychological factors that predispose some individuals and societies to reactions of extreme hostility and hatred directed towards racial and religious groups. The writings of Theodor Adorno, Bruno Bettelheim, Morris Janowitz, Seymour Martin Lipset, Alan Davies, Gordon Allport, Charles Stember, Rodney Stark, and Harold Quinley are indicative of the vast social science research that has been done in this area.[17]

In particular, Glock and Stark, in *Christian Beliefs and Anti–Semitism*, propounded a correlation between those professing anti–

Semitic beliefs and their Christian beliefs and affiliation. Gary Marx's *Protest and Prejudice* found blacks no more anti-Semitic than whites; to the extent that black anti-Semitism exists, it results largely from unfavorable social and economic contact between Jew and black.[18]

The Tenacity of Prejudice, a survey analysis by Selznick and Steinberg, isolates the independent variables that contribute to anti-Semitism. The researchers developed an "Index of Anti-Semitic Belief," which they submitted to 2,000 respondents. Analyzing the results, they found that education, more than age, generation, geographical location, and religious beliefs, was the most important independent variable in determining the extent of anti-Semitic bias. They went on to predict the gradual disappearance of anti-Semitism with the spread of education.[19]

Anti-Semitism in the United States: A Study of Prejudice in the 1980s, by Gregory Martire and Ruth Clark, is very much in the same tradition. Also using survey analysis, the authors attempt to provide "the first comprehensive trend study of anti-Semitism in the United States, and...to examine the factors that are associated with American anti-Semitism in the 1980s."[20] Drawing on the Selznick and Steinberg study, plus a 1977 study on attitudes towards Israel by Yankelovich, Skelly, and White, Inc., Martire and Clark conducted 50 in-depth interviews with Jews and non-Jews from across the nation and compiled a quantitative survey based on 1,215 personal interviews representing all adult groupings in the contiguous United States.

The authors conclude that although a minority, "individuals holding anti-Semitic beliefs clearly represent a significant social problem in the United States."[21] One in four (23 percent) non-Jews can be characterized as prejudiced. Though anti-Semitic beliefs continue to present a serious problem, the authors found a decline since 1964 in the prevalence of many traditional anti-Semitic stereotypes, such as negative images relating to shrewdness, dishonesty, assertiveness, or willingness to use shady business practices. The decline results not from changes in the attitudes of individuals, but rather from generational change—the coming of age of those who were children in the mid-1960s, who as young people tended to be relatively unprejudiced and who showed an increased tolerance of diversity.

Martire and Clark did not find any particular correlation among political conservatism, energy crisis concerns, dual loyalty fears, or religious fundamentalism and anti-Semitism. Instead, their study indicates that anti-Semitism is associated most strongly with three demographic characteristics: age, education, and race. "The level of anti-Semitism is higher among adults who are older, less educated, or black."[22] After controlling for education, however, they found that young adults are significantly less anti-Semitic than those who are older, thus pointing to the generational variable as the most important determinant. This finding has a number of significant implications for the authors. "It suggests that an individual's attitude towards Jews is probably relatively enduring.... It also suggests that the decline in anti-Semitism should continue as the better-educated and more tolerant young adults continue through the life cycle...."[23]

The only exception to this hopeful prognosis is the black community. The authors found that race is the other demographic factor most closely associated with anti-Semitism. About 23 percent of whites can be characterized as prejudiced compared to 37 percent of blacks.[24] Black anti-Semitism appears to stem primarily from the tensions caused by the middleman minority, or retailer-consumer, relationship that characterizes the economic interactions of the two groups.[25]

Notwithstanding that these studies have made an important contribution to the growing body of social science literature on the subject of anti-Semitism, some weaknesses in the approach need highlighting. Since such studies lack a historical orientation and because, as Lucy Dawidowicz pointed out in an important article in *Commentary,* of "its single focus on opinion," the survey analysis method is "not properly geared to study the etiology of anti-Semitism. Useful for periodic pulse-taking, it nevertheless serves ultimately to limit our understanding of anti-Semitism, which is a phenomenon marked by a high degree of multiformity and contradictoriness."[26] Furthermore, these works of social research do not explain the earlier and specifically American manifestations of anti-Semitism.

During the late 1940s, Carey McWilliams attempted a historical perspective with the thesis that racial prejudice was primarily the product of economic factors. According to McWilliams, the industrial barons fomented anti-Semitism to provide "a mask for privilege" enabling them to exploit without detection a society that professed democratic ideals. This rationalization for their elite social order came into being with the rise of industrial capitalism in the late nineteenth century.[27]

McWilliams's use of Marxist theory to explain American anti-Semitism, although provocative, lost favor in the following decade with the rise of another intellectual deity—consensus. Historians in the late 1950s carried out an extensive grading process to smooth over America's social convulsions. They emphasized the continuity and homogeneity of American history, the stability of basic institutions, and the nonideological, conservative nature of political and social life. They minimized the importance of the myths and stereotypes that have exacerbated the differences between competing groups and, instead, they idealized their surface uniformity and agreement. This historical tendency has characterized the most accepted scholarship on American anti-Semitism. Although porous and far from definitive, the accepted scholarship has succeeded in generating a sense of well-being and tolerance that has not done justice to the evidence.

Oscar Handlin, one of the early proponents of this school, argued that capitalistic economic organization had very little to do with inducing prejudice against any group; including Jews. He also pointed out that the plutocrats were not the only ones who may have fomented prejudice, but that liberal thinkers often were tainted with anti-Semitism as well. In contrast to the Marxist interpretation, Handlin generally de-emphasized the scope of anti-Semitism in the nineteenth century and argued instead that by 1900 there existed a prevailing temper of tolerance and a great willingness to accept the Jew.[28] American anti-Semitism was a transitory phenomenon resulting from a multiplicity of social pressures: mass immigration, rapid industrialization, the depression of the nineties and the agrarian discontent of the late nineteenth century. Handlin further asserts that the American stereotypes involved no hostility, no negative judgment, and were not taken as such at the time.[29] The recent work of Naomi Cohen indicates that this clearly was not the case.[30]

Historian John Higham, cognizant of the weaknesses inherent in the panoramic approach of consensus historiography, nevertheless emphasized a causal relationship that, if followed to its conclusion, and removing certain social ingredients, would belie the significance of the nativist phenomenon.[31] He argued that anti-Semitism essentially was caused by the tensions resulting from a genuine conflict of interests between competing social, economic, or ethnic groups. Further, he held that the first great acceleration of American anti-Semitism occurred in the post-Civil War period, continuing until the turn of the century, when an aspiring first- and second-generation Jewish community rapidly began to impinge upon the social preserve of their native American neighbors. Discrimination developed wherever Jews participated in the middle-class scramble for prestige and status; it developed "where and when a hectic pace of social climbing made the guardians of distinction afraid of being invaded."[32] American anti-Semitism, Higham contended, owes little to ideological sources. Nor does stereotypic thinking play a decisive role. Actual, everyday conflicts in the social and economic arenas provided the patterns of exclusion that gradually restricted the opportunities of American Jews.[33]

Higham denied the contention of Oscar Handlin and Cary McWilliams that discrimination grew as reactionary leaders imposed their undemocratic values on the innocent masses. He also criticized Richard Hofstadter and Handlin for focusing too much attention on the role of ideas and images and not enough attention on economic forces.[34]

The 1915 lynching of Leo Frank in Georgia was the most prominent anti-Semitic event in American history. Leonard Dinnerstein's

The Leo Frank Case, undoubtedly the finest analysis of any American anti-Semitic incident, relates the arrest, trial, and lynching of Frank to Southern social and economic tensions caused by rapid industrialization and urbanization of an unprepared rural population. According to Dinnerstein, fundamentalist Southern migrants found it extremely difficult to adjust to the urban tempo of Atlanta and other burgeoning Southern cities; therefore, they lashed out at a symbol of foreignness and social change, the Jew.[35]

Arnold Rose's famous essay, "Anti-Semitism's Root in City Hatred," attributes American anti-Semitism to identification of the Jews with the cities during a period when anti-urbanism was rife. The Jews' association with political radicalism, economic success, and cultural modernism stemmed from their residence in the large cities, especially New York.[36] For Rose, Dinnerstein, Handlin, and Higham, anti-Semitism, rather than being an ever-present phenomenon expressed in ideological and religious forms, has resulted from a unique mix of social and economic factors coming together at particular historical moments.

Beginning in the late 1960s, American scholars apparently became more sensitive to the issue of American anti-Semitism and the role of ideology. Critical of the grading-over process of consensus historiography, they initiated a revisionist critique of the problem. Several factors account for this development. American historians of the time engaged generally in a critical rethinking of assumptions long taken for granted concerning the political, economic, and social realities of our past. American Jewish scholars, just beginning to come into their own in academia, were drawn towards aspects of the American Jewish experience previously unexamined. The pluralistic attitudes characteristic of 1960s culture brought Jews and Jewish scholars out of the closet, so to speak, and made it easier for them to publicly discuss issues of Jewish concern. The growing interest in the Holocaust, spurred on by the 1962 Eichmann trial, the 1967 Arab-Israeli war and predictions of a second Holocaust, and the emergence of Elie Wiesel as folk hero and witness to atrocity generated interest in the problem of anti-Semitism.

In addition, Israel's creation in 1948 had posed theological problems for many Christians. These people believed that Judaism ceased as a creative and legitimate force with the rise of Christianity, and that the destruction of the Temple in 70 B.C.E. had marked the death of Judaism and the Jewish people as viable, living entities. The perception that Jews were "a fossilized relic of Syriac society," as British historian Arnold Toynbee put it, apparently made it difficult for many Christians to support the modern state created by this "anachronistic" people.[37] Yet these factors, one can surmise, facilitated a renewed interest in Jewish-Christian relations in America and the desire to look closely and critically at the problem of American anti–Semitism.

Elsewhere I have challenged the conventional wisdom in this area on two grounds: that anti–Semitism has been far more important and pervasive in our national history than previous scholars were willing to admit, and that the persistence of anti–Semitism over time in different social and economic contexts throws some doubt on the socio-economic explanation of its existence. Instead, I draw attention to the role of stereotypes in perpetuating negative attitudes towards Jews.

In an important essay on the image of the Jew in German popular literature, the eminent historian of German anti–Semitism, George Mosse, urges his readers "to direct their attention to cultural investigation." It was Mosse's contention that "only in this way will we be able to understand better the continued influence of anti–Semitism which...seems to predate and outlast its immediate political and social relevance." Similarly, Jean–Paul Sartre focused on "the idea of the Jew" as the generating factor of anti–Semitism.[38]

I have identified eight images for consideration: the Jew as eternal enemy of Christianity, the Jewish criminal, the deceitful Shylock, the parvenu, the eternal alien, the international conspirator, the quintessential captitalist, and the prototypical radical. These images were staples of newspaper and magazine articles, plays, and the dime novels. They were perpetuated by both the famous and unknown of the American literary scene. Perhaps the most unsettling aspect of this pervasive negative imagery is the acute depersonalization of the American Jew that the stereotypical literature helped to achieve. Jews became figures merely reified into objects, stripped of their individuality to fit the stereotyped roles expected of them, thus exacerbating the pressures among real–life Jews to assimilate.

This phenomenon corresponds closely to the situation in Germany during the Third Reich, when National Socialism incited hatred of the Jews by evolving a stereotypical image devoid of real or human characteristics in the popular mind. This permitted many Germans to claim a Jewish friend who was not like "those other Jews." Obviously, anti–Semitism in America during the late nineteenth and twentieth centuries never evolved into the terrible ending engendered by its European counterparts. At least with respect to image we did not have far to go.[39]

Nineteenth–century American society probably was unaware of the European historical background that had built anti–Semitism into its societal structure. Except for a few knowledgeable individuals, Americans hardly knew of the medieval ecclesiastical statutes limiting the types of economic activity available to Jews. Consequently, while the origins of the structurally created anti–Semitism in European and American society had been forgotten, the symbolic expressions of these origins remained imbedded in the literature and sensibilities of Western society in the form of pejorative stereotypes.[40]

What is the relationship of these images to the tendency to discriminate against Jews? Do all negative images lead inevitably to discrimination? Are some more dangerous than others? What elements in society benefit from discrimination? What impact have these negative images had on Jewish self–perception and self–esteem? Has their existence fostered the rush towards assimilation?

Among the relatively few books and articles that examine American anti–Semitism from a historical perspective, one finds only tentative answers to these questions. The best known works—the studies by Handlin, Higham, Rose, Dinnerstein (*The Leo Frank Case*), McWilliams, and Hofstadter—argue that anti–Semitism is the consequence of objective socio–economic factors and tensions operative in society that affect marginal groups.[41] Recently Diamond and Ribuffo have extended this analysis of social conflict to include those individuals who have created or joined radical right and Christian right organizations.[42]

Before we can generalize about their findings, we need to know why certain individuals are attracted to extremist movements. As William Schneider has recently pointed out, Joseph McCarthy, George Wallace, and more recent right wing ideologues such as Jerry Falwell have not been associated openly with anti–Semitic sentiments: "These right–wing figures...conscientiously avoided the exploitation of anti–Semitism among their followers. Indeed, some candidates of the New Right have made explicit overtures to Jews, arguing that Jews should consider their self–interest and not merely their ideology."[43]

Similarly, it is not enough to say, for example, that all fundamentalists are anti–Semitic. As Ribuffo has argued, there is "no necessary connection between conservative theology and far right activism... nevertheless, the convention associating fundamentalism with bigotry and reaction, created during the 1920s, was widely disseminated.... Following World War II, this convention, combined with surfacing suspicion of 'simple folk,' would decisively influence interpretations of the far right."[44] In their recent study of anti–Semitism in America, Martire and Clark have concluded, in fact,

> that the relationship between Christian orthodoxy and anti–Semitism is due almost entirely to three demographic factors: education, race, and age....After controlling for education, race, and age, we find that the partial correlation between religiousness and anti–Semitism virtually disappears, indicating that the apparent relationship is actually due to the fact that individuals who are traditional in their religious outlook are more likely to be older, less educated, and black—all factors that are associated with higher levels of anti–Semitic belief.[45]

Finally, anti–Semitic ideology and anti–Semitic attitudes are insufficient in themselves to explain America's anti–Jewish tendencies. Most contemporary analyses of American anti–Semitism show, disturbingly, that in the late nineteenth and early twentieth centuries, anti–Semitism was separated from analysis of capitalist development, thereby locating the American–Jewish problem in a structural vacuum independent from other economic or social tendencies.

Much valuable work has been done on the effect of image, ideology, and myth on the development of American anti–Semitism. However, there has been insufficient reflection on socio–economic factors independent of ethnic, religious, or national characteristics. We know, for example, from sociological literature, that there is a well-established tendency as economic competition increases, albeit real or imagined, for ethnic antagonisms to increase among competing discernible groups. Richard Rubenstein has pointed out this phenomenon in *The Cunning of History*. This is true for wage–labor conflicts, certain economic dependency relationships, or business competition.[46] Max Weber cites the antagonisms that can result if a particular group is identified with a particular economic activity or position such as debtor or creditor.[47] Similarly, sociologists Wallimann and Bonacich have observed antagonism between retailers and consumers when the two tended to belong to different ethnic groups.[48]

In fact, there is a growing sociological literature on "middleman minorities" and victimization. Were such mechanisms also present in the American–Jewish situation? Was the Jewish community in any way discernible as a competitor of non–Jewish segments of the American society, and could it as such be targeted for political exploitation by a rising anti–Semitic movement? David Gerber suggests this was the case in ante–bellum Buffalo, New York.[49] Recent studies indicate that this may also be operative in the rising tide of anti–Semitism among blacks. As Gary Marx and others have argued, evidence suggests that, because of their own historically marginal status, Jews have developed a "middleman" role between the black community and white society, in roles such as teachers, principals, merchants, social workers, and doctors. Thus Marx concludes convincingly: "While we do not assume that these contacts are the sole source of Negro hostility, it would seem from the data that they are an important source."[50]

So what do we have here? It is true that many immigrant groups underwent attack in America. And it must be said that Jews neither met with as much hostility nor as much acceptance as did certain other minorities. Rapid social and economic advancement, although exposing Jews to more social discrimination, also left them in a better position to deal with it. Once they emerged from the ghettos into the suburbs in the second generation, their newly attained economic positions, educational levels, and emerging defense organizations served as cushions to deflate raw prejudice. In fact, their remarkable success in America, a source of mixed admiration and envy, weakened the potential impact of anti–Semitism. Jews, as John Higham has indicated, did not fall victim to as much violence as did the Italians or Chinese. They were not subject to as much discrimination as were blacks. And there was no organized anti–Semitic movement comparable to the anti–Catholic American Protective Association. "The relative mildness of American, as compared to European anti–Semitism must be attributed not only to the more tolerant traditions of the United States... but also to the presence within the country of a great variety of ethnic and [racial] targets. Nevertheless a good deal of distinctively anti–Semitic sentiment also emerged."[51]

The fact is anti–Semitism erupted even in reformist and libertarian sectors of American society. The democratic impulse was not and may not be always resolute enough to overcome the psychological and social momentum of anti–Semitic stereotyping.[52] True, America never visited mass physical oppression upon its Jews. But there are more subtle types of oppression—economic, social, and cultural—that are also damaging and painful. In addition to the ideological factors, John Higham has drawn attention to the serious problem of social discrimination against Jews. "The highly publicized exclusion of Joseph Seligman, one of the leading American bankers, from the Grand Union Hotel in Saratoga in 1877" brought notice to a trend already well under way. Saratoga, Nahant, Newport, Long Branch, Lakewood, even New York City, soon became battlegrounds. Signs like "No Jews or Dogs Admitted Here" were common in many of America's finest resorts. Rather than accept this, some prominent Jews, like Nathan Straus, retaliated by buying several of the leading hotels that excluded Jews.[53]

Discrimination at summer resorts, private schools, and clubs increased during the years before World War I. The Century Club in New York rejected the distinguished scientist Jacques Loeb because he was a Jew. Most Masonic lodges excluded Jews. Some of the most prestigious preparatory schools, such as Exeter, Hotchkiss, and Andover, had small Jewish quotas. After 1900, few Jews were elected to the Princeton clubs or to the fraternities at Yale, Columbia, and Harvard. The literary and gymnastic societies at Columbia kept Jews out entirely. As a result, Jewish students gradually formed their own fraternities, the first appearing at Columbia in 1898. The anti–Semitic feelings also infected college faculties. It was common knowledge that few Jews could gain entry or advancement in American academic circles.[54]

Social discrimination reached a climax in the quota systems adopted by colleges and medical schools in the years after World War I. Many colleges set limits on Jewish enrollment. Some established alumni committees to screen applicants. Others, under the pretext of seeking regional balance, gave preference to students outside the East, thereby limiting the number of Jews, who were heavily concentrated there. The most common method of exclusion came with the introduction of character and psychological examinations.

Before the 1920s, scholastic performance was the most important criteria used in admissions policies. Now admissions committees devised tests to rank students on such characteristics as "public spirit," "fair play," "interest in fellows," and "leadership," traits not usually associated with Jews in the popular mind. By 1919 New York University instituted stringent restrictions and introduced psychological testing. Chancellor Elmor Brown justified this policy, citing the "separateness" of the Jewish student body.[55] Dean Archibald Lewis Bouton, probably the premier exponent of this position within the university, elaborated on the chancellor's theme: "A grave condition...affects the efficiency of the entire process of training when...the student body is made up of large masses of students who segregate themselves into groups exactly as in the city outside...."[56] Columbia University cut the number of Jews in the incoming classes from 40 to 20 percent. At Harvard, where elite Protestant students and faculty feared the university's becoming a "new Jerusalem," President A. Lawrence Lowell in 1922 recommended a quota system, openly adopting what other institutions were doing covertly. "There is...a rapidly growing anti-Semitic feeling in this country," he wrote in June of that year, "caused by...a strong race feeling on the part of the Jews."[57] Smaller colleges, perhaps more rigid than some large, urban ones, used more subjective criteria, such as requiring a photograph of the candidate and enforcing a geographic distribution. This was even a greater problem in medical schools, where formidable barriers spread throughout the country, severely limiting Jewish enrollments and causing undue hardship.[58]

The most significant ideological attack against Jews also occurred during the 1920s. It focused not on religious issues or Jewish social climbing but on race and political subversion. A resurgent Ku Klux Klan activated the old myths about Jews as Christ killers and race polluters. More significantly, the country witnessed the resurrection of the international stereotype of the Jew as half banker and half Bolshevik, conspiring to seize control of the nation. This belief, having been foreshadowed during the Civil War and emerged in the 1890s during the Populist ferment, crystalized in the early 1920s around auto magnate Henry Ford. In May of 1922, Ford's newspaper, the Dearborn *Independent*, launched an anti-Semitic propaganda campaign without precedent in American history. It lasted for about seven years. In time, the newspaper "exposed" Jewish control of everything from the League of Nations to American politics, from baseball and jazz to agriculture and movies. The *Independent* claimed that the press was owned, slanted, and muzzled by Jewish money;

that Jews were corrupting the labor movement with socialist ideas; that they were infiltrating the churches with higher criticism and liberalism; that they were infecting the youth of America with corruption and sin. If any pattern of ideas activated discrimination, it was the conspiratorial ferment to which the Populists, Henry Ford, and the KKK contributed.[59]

With the approach of World War II, these issues were further clouded by events in Europe. As Hitler proved to be virulently anti–Semitic, American Jews began to argue for intervention in the affairs of Europe, a stand resented by isolationists committed to keeping America out of the impending conflagration. On September 11, 1941, American aviation hero Charles Lindbergh warned that the Jews and President Roosevelt were conspiring to bring the nation into a war against Germany and that such a war would prove catastrophic for America.

The situation became more acute when European Jews began to seek refuge in this country. The growing isolationism and xenophobia of the 1930s, as well as public opinion polls of the periods, have shown how stereotyping reinforced insensitivity and misunderstanding and contributed to governmental inertia in the face of an unprecedented human tragedy. The critical decade of the 1930s witnessed the rise of Nazism in Europe, as well as a high degree of acceptance and approval of anti–Semitism in America. Although sympathetic to the plight of the refugees, many Americans remained unalterably opposed to admitting them. Even Jewish children were not exempt from the public opposition to raising immigration quotas.

There seems to be a correlation between this insensitivity and the public's perception of Jews. This sentiment undoubtedly reinforced the isolationist bent in the Congress, making it extremely difficult to liberalize laws on immigration quotas to admit more Jewish refugees. The roots of this apathy and hostility indeed may have been nurtured in the anti–Semitic milieu that characterized the preceding decades.[60]

Many of the difficulties refugees encountered could be attributed to the subjectivity of American consular officials in Europe and to bureaucratic red tape. The potential immigrant had to present an unexpired passport or police certificate attesting to good conduct in the past, a certificate from a public health official, duplicate records of all pertinent personal data (birth, marriage, and divorce certificates), and a thorough financial statement, as well as an affidavit filed by a guarantor, some relative or friend in America, describing his or her complete assets and naming the specific percentage of support intended for the applicant. One improper entry among the volume of fifty or so pages of documents could result in rejection or further delays when each day might prove vital. As one can imagine, much of this documentation was difficult if not impossible to obtain by Jews in Hitler's Germany. Consequently, only approximately 127,000 refugees, or on the average a little over 18,000 a year, came to the United States between 1933 and 1940. Without congressional action, 183,112 could have entered the U.S. from Germany and Austria. Obstructions and red tape kept out at least 60,000 deserving others.[61]

These practical hurdles confronting the refugee who desired to come to America were reinforced by a more subjective obstacle. Powerful restrictionist sentiment throughout most of the country prevailed in Congress and was intensfied by the proliferation of nativist anti–Semitism. The majority of the American people, including many liberal and labor leaders, as Barbara Stewart has argued, opposed the reform of existing immigration laws and regulations. Anti–refugee and anti–immigration campaigns were conducted in nationwide publications throughout this period, accusing refugees of being wealthy, parvenu, conspicuous consumers. This group, it was charged, had not only "taken over" exclusive hotels, "overrun" fashionable resorts, and "paraded" in expensive restaurants and nightclubs, but it was attempting to shape American cultural and intellectual life and had often behaved in an arrogant, self–assertive, ostentatious, and rude manner.[62] From 1934 to 1937, *The Saturday Evening Post* published numerous editorials and articles demanding immigration restriction, a notable statistic since George Horace Larimer's magazine had a 1937 circulation of three million copies a week, higher than any magazine ever had achieved.[63] Arguing that the number of foreigners in the United States must be cut because of unemployment, the writers placed even more emphasis on the undesirability of most refugees.

This sentiment fed into a form of Catholic anti–Semitism best represented by Father Charles Coughlin, who spoke for the beliefs of small–town America. Beginning in 1936, in his journal, *Social Justice*, and on his widely aired radio broadcasts (with 20 to 30 million listeners), he began to argue that European fascism was a legitimate response to the more pernicious threat of communism that was largely inspired by Jews. His diatribes continued until 1942, when he was finally taken off the air. However, Fritz Kuhn's German–American Bund, Gerald L.K. Smith, Dudley Pelley, and other pro–Nazi and anti–Semitic groups and individuals kept the issue alive.

Two public opinion surveys—one conducted before the *Anschluss* in March 1938, the other after *Kristallnacht* in November—demonstrate how little even these two shocking events affected people's attitudes towards refugees. Roughly the same percentage thought that refugees should not be admitted. Asked in the first poll, "What is your attitude toward allowing German, Austrian and other political refugees to come into the United States?" 4.9 percent responded that we should encourage them to come even if we have to raise the immigration quotas; an additional 18.2 percent thought we should allow them to come in but not raise the immigration quotas (totalling 23.1 percent in favor of refugee immigration); 67.4 percent said that under current conditions we should try to keep them out. Asked in the poll of November 22, "Should we allow a large number of Jewish exiles from Germany to come to the United States to live?" 23 percent said yes and 77 percent said no.[64] A 1939 *Fortune* poll asked, "If you were a member of Congress would you vote yes or no on a bill to open the doors of the United States to a larger number of refugees than are now admitted under our immigration quotas?" Only 8.7 percent replied yes and 83 percent no.[65] The message was clear: refugees were not wanted.

When you add up all the individual cases of American anti–Semitism they may not seem very significant. But when viewed differently, the callous lack of concern for Nazi refugees and refusal to admit them that led to certain death for countless thousands becomes painfully disturbing. Although America may have been different, it was not different enough.

Notes

1. Emil Fackenheim, *The Jewish Return into History* (New York: Schocken Books, 1978), p. 152.

2. Ibid., p. 155.

3. Ibid., pp. 155–156.

4. John Higham, *Send These to Me* (New York: Atheneum, 1975), p. 174.

5. See Jacob Katz, *Exclusiveness and Tolerance* (New York: Schocken Books, 1962); Jacob Katz, *From Prejudice to Destruction: Anti–Semitism, 1700–1933* (Cambridge: Harvard University Press, 1980); H.H. Ben–Sasson and S. Ettinger, eds., *Jewish Society Through the Ages* (London: Vallentine, Mitchell, 1971); Edward Flannery, *The Anguish of the Jews* (New York: Macmillan, 1965); Uriel Tal, *Christians and Jews in Germany: Religion, Politics and Ideology in the Second Reich, 1870–1914*, trans. Noah J. Jacobs (Ithaca, New York: Cornell University Press, 1975); Joshua Trachtenberg, *The Devil and the Jews: The Medieval Conception of the Jew and Its Relation to Anti–Semitism* (New Haven, Conn.: Yale University Press, 1944); Yehuda Bauer, *A History of the Holocaust* (New York: F. Watts, 1982); Jean–Paul Sartre, *Anti–Semite and Jew* (New York: Schocken Books, 1965); and George Mosse, *The Crisis of German Ideology* (New York: Grossett and Dunlap, 1964).

6. Higham, *Send These to Me*, p. 116.

7. Particularly important works on American anti–Semitism include Michael Dobkowski, *The Tarnished Dream: The Basis of American Anti–Semitism* (Westport, Conn.: Greenwood Press, 1979); Leonard Dinnerstein, *The Leo Frank Case* (New York: Columbia University Press, 1968); Naomi W. Cohen, *Not Free to Desist: The American Jewish Committee, 1906–1966* (Philadelphia: The Jewish Publication Society of America, 1972); Saul Friedman,

The Incident at Massena (New York: Stein and Day, 1978); Marcia Graham Synnott, *The Half-Opened Door: Discrimination and Admissions at Harvard, Yale, and Princeton, 1900–1970* (Westport, Conn.: Greenwood Press, 1979); Harold S. Wechsler, *The Qualified Student: A History of Selective College Admission in America* (New York: Wiley, 1977); Albert Lee, *Henry Ford and the Jews* (New York: Stein and Day, 1980). While not strictly about anti–Semitism, rich sources of documentary evidence are Morris U. Schappes, *Documentary History of the Jews in the United States, 1654–1875* (New York: Citadel Press, 1950), which also has a helpful introduction, and Louis Harap, *The Image of the Jew in American Literature* (Philadelphia: The Jewish Publication Society of America, 1974). Useful articles have been produced by Leonard Dinnerstein, Leo Ribuffo, Arnold Rose, Morris U. Schappes, Robert Rockaway, David Gerber, William F. Holmes, and a number of other scholars.

8. Higham, *Send These to Me*, p. 138.

9. See Harap, *The Image of the Jew*, pp. 3–16.

10. Ben Halpern, "What is Anti–Semitism?" *Modern Judaism* 1, no. 3 (December 1981): 251–262.

11. See John Higham, *Strangers in the Land* (New Brunswick, N.J.: Rutgers University Press, 1953).

12. Jonathan Sarna, "Anti–Semitism and American History," *Commentary* 17 (March 1981): 42–47.

13. John Higham, *Send These to Me*, p. 121.

14. Lee J. Levinger's *Anti–Semitism in the United States: Its History and Causes* (New York: Bloch, 1925) was a popular study of current events.

15. Walter Lippmann, *Public Opinion* (New York: Penguin Books, 1946); Horace Kallen, *Culture and Democracy in the United States* (New York: Boni and Liveright, 1924). See Ronald A. Urquhart, "The American Reaction to the Dreyfus Affair: A Study of Anti–Semitism in the 1890s" (Ph.D. diss., Columbia University, 1972).

16. Gardiner Murphy, L.B. Murphy, and Theodore Newcomb, *Experimental Social Psychology* (New York: Harper and Brothers, 1937), pp. 889–1,046; David Krech and Richard S. Crutchfield, *Theory and Problems of Social Psychology* (New York: McGraw–Hill, 1948), p. 487. See Urquhart, "The American Reaction to Dreyfus," as well.

17. See Theodor Adorno et al., *The Authoritarian Personality* (New York: Harper and Brothers, 1950); Bruno Bettelheim and Morris Janowitz, *Dynamics of Prejudice* (New York: Harper and Brothers, 1950); Seymour Martin Lipset, *The Politics of Unreason* (New York: Harper and Row, 1970); Alan T. Davies, *Anti–Semitism and the Christian Mind* (New York: Herder and Herder, 1969); Gordon Allport, *The Nature of Prejudice* (Cambridge, Mass.: Addison–Wesley, 1954); Charles Stember, *Jews in the Mind of America* (New

York: Basic Books, 1966); Charles Y. Glock and Rodney Stark, *Christian Beliefs and Anti-Semitism* (New York: Harper and Row, 1966); Harold Quinley and Charles Y. Glock, *Anti-Semitism in America* (New York: Free Press, 1979); Gregory Martire and Ruth Clark, *Anti-Semitism in the United States: A Study of Prejudice in the 1980s* (New York: Praeger, 1982). See also Urquhart, "The American Reaction to Dreyfus."

18. Gary G. Marx, *Protest and Prejudice* (New York: Harper and Row, 1969).

19. Gertrude J. Selznick and Stephen Steinberg, *The Tenacity of Prejudice* (New York: Harper and Row, 1969).

20. Martire and Clark, *Anti-Semitism in the U.S.*, p. 3.

21. Ibid., p. 4.

22. Ibid., p. 44.

23. Ibid., p. 116.

24. Ibid., p. 45.

25. See Edna Bonacich, "A Theory of Ethnic Antagonism: The Split Labor Market," *American Sociological Review* 37 (October 1972): 547–549.

26. Lucy Dawidowicz, *The Jewish Presence* (New York: Holt, Rinehart and Winston, 1977), p. 212.

27. Cary McWilliams, *A Mask for Privilege: Anti-Semitism in America* (Boston: Little, Brown and Co., 1948). See Urquhart, "The American Reaction to Dreyfus."

28. See Urquhart, "The American Reaction to Dreyfus," pp. iii–v.

29. See Oscar Handlin, "American Views of the Jew at the Opening of the Twentieth Century," *Publications of the American Jewish Historical Society* 40 (June 1951): 324–345; and Handlin, "How United States Anti-Semitism Really Began: Its Grass-Roots Source in the 90's," *Commentary* 2, no. 6 (June 1951): 542–543.

30. Naomi W. Cohen, "Anti-Semitism in the Gilded Age: The Jewish View," *Jewish Social Studies* 41 (Summer–Fall 1979): 187–210.

31. John Higham, "The Cult of the 'American Consensus': Homogenizing Our History," *Commentary* 27 (February 1959): 93–100.

32. John Higham, "Another Look at Nativism," *The Catholic Review* 44, no. 2 (July 1958): 154.

33. Even Higham's revised essays in *Send These to Me* continued to de-emphasize the impact of ideology.

34. John Higham, "Anti-Semitism in the Gilded Age: A Reinterpretation," *Mississippi Valley Historical Review* 43, no. 4 (March 1957): 559–578; and John Higham, "Social Discrimination against Jews in America, 1830–1930," *Publications of the American Jewish Historical Society* 47 (September 1957–June 1958): 1–33. See Harap, *The Image of the Jew.*

35. Leonard Dinnerstein, *The Leo Frank Case.*

36. Arnold Rose, "Anti-Semitism's Roots in City Hatred," *Commentary* 6 (1948): 374–378.

37. Arnold Toynbee, *A Study of History*, vol. 1 (London: Oxford University Press, 1934), p. 90.

38. The importance of this concept is noted in an anonymous review in *American Jewish Archives* 31, no. 2 (November 1979): 220–221.

39. Ibid.

40. See Urquhart, "The American Reaction to Dreyfus," p. viii.

41. See Richard Hofstadter, *Age of Reform* (New York: Vintage Books, 1960), pp. 92–93; and Hofstadter, *Social Darwinism in American Thought* (Boston: Beacon Press, 1955), p. 176.

42. See Sander Diamond, *The Nazi Movement in the United States: 1924–1941* (Ithaca, N.Y.: Cornell University Press, 1974); Leo Ribuffo, "Henry Ford and the International Jew," *American Jewish History* 69 (June 1980): 437–477; and Ribuffo, *The Old Christian Right* (Philadelphia: Temple University Press, 1983).

43. William Schneider, quoted in Martire and Clark, *Anti-Semitism in the United States*, pp. 63–64.

44. Ribuffo, *The Old Christian Right*, p. 181.

45. Martire and Clark, *Anti-Semitism in the United States*, pp. 74–75.

46. See Richard Rubenstein, *The Cunning of History* (New York: Harper and Row, 1975).

47. Max Weber, *The Theory of Social and Economic Organizations*, ed. Talcott Parsons (Glencoe, Ill.: Free Press, 1957).

48. Isidor Wallimann, "Towards a Theoretical Understanding of Ethnic Antagonism: The Case of the Foreign Workers in Switzerland," *Zeitschrift fur Soziologie* 3, no. 1 (February 1974): 84–94; Edna Bonacich, "A Theory of Ethnic Antagonism: The Split Labor Market," pp. 547–549; and Bonacich, "A Theory of Middleman Minorities," *American Sociological Review* 38 (October 1973): 583–594.

49. David Gerber, "Cutting Out Shylock," *The Journal of American History* 69, no. 3 (December 1982): 615–630.

50. Marx, *Protest and Prejudice*, pp. 154, 165–166. See also Martire and Clark, *Anti-Semitism in the United States*, pp. 44–45, 51–52.

51. John Higham, *Send These to Me*, p. 130.

52. Ibid., pp. 131–135.

53. Ibid., pp. 148–149.

54. Ibid., pp. 150–152.

55. *New York University Daily News* 1, no. 82 (May 11, 1923): 4.

56. *New York University Alumnus* 1, no. 2 (November 1920): 24.

57. A. Lawrence Lowell to A.C. Ratshevsky, June 7, 1922, American Jewish Committee Archives, General Correspondence, 1906–1932 (New York), folder D–E, s.v. "discrimination."

58. Higham, pp. 159–162.

59. Ibid., pp. 169–172, 187–188.

60. See Barbara M. Stewart, "United States Government Policy on Refugees from Nazism, 1933–1940" (Ph.D. dissertation, Columbia University, 1969), pp. 7–14.

61. See Saul Friedman, *No Haven for the Oppressed* (Detroit: Wayne State University Press, 1973); Henry Feingold, *The Politics of Rescue* (New Brunswick, N.J.: Rutgers University Press, 1970): Arthur D. Morse, *While Six Million Died* (New York: Hart Publishing, 1967); David Wyman, *Paper Walls* (Boston: University of Massachusetts Press, 1968); Wyman, *The Abandonment of the Jews* (New York: Pantheon Books, 1984); Walter Laqueur, *The Terrible* Secret (Boston: Little, Brown, and Co., 1980); Michael Dobkowski, *The Politics of Indifference* (Washington, D.C.: University Press of America, 1982); and Stewart, "U.S. Policy on Refugees from Nazism."

62. Emily Post, "The Refugees," *New York Herald Tribune*, May 28, 1944; S.F. Porter, "Refugee Gold Rush," *American Magazine* 134 (October 1942): 46–47; "Rules for Refugees, Royal or Otherwise, While in America," *Life*, December 16, 1940, p. 91.

63. "The Fortune Quarterly Survey," *Fortune* 18 (July 1938): 20; Hadley Cantril, Milder Strank, eds., *Public Opinion: 1935–1946* (Princeton: Princeton University Press, 1951), p. 385; "The Fortune Quarterly Survey," *Fortune* 19 (April 1939): 102–104; Stewart, "U.S. Policy on Refugees from Nazism," p. 237.

64. "The Fortune Quarterly Survey," *Fortune* 18 (July 1938): 80; Cantril and Strank, eds., *Public Opinion: 1935–1946*, p. 385; Stewart, "U.S. Policy on Refugees from Nazism," pp. 360–361.

65. "The Fortune Quarterly Survey," *Fortune* 19 (April 1939): 102–104; Stewart, "U.S. Policy on Refugees from Nazism," pp. 361–362.

Chapter 5

More Devils Than Hell Can Hold:
Anti–Semitism in American Literature

Carole Kessner

An oblique but illuminating approach to the complex subject of anti–Semitism in American literature involves a riddle that has at least two answers. Question: When is anti–Semitism not anti–Semitism? Answer 1: When it is not listed in the *Oxford English Dictionary*, that definitive etymological lexicon of the English language. (Its inclusion in the *American College Dictionary* published by Random House counters this fact.) Answer 2: When it is either anti–Judaism or anti–Zionism. Strictly speaking, the latter is also correct, once we clarify a few terms. Though on the deepest level the distinctions are merely semantic, there is a vital link among them.

The word *anti–Semitism* was not coined until the middle of the nineteenth century when a German journalist of small note, Wilhelm Marr, added it to the vocabulary of then current pseudoscientific social theories.[1] These racial postulates, derived from the anthropology and linguistics of the day, purported to explain the essential differences between Aryans and Semites. "'History proves that Semites do not possess the psychical forces that distinguish the Aryans,' wrote Christian Lassen, a German professor of ancient civilizations." But the Semite does have other characteristics. He is "selfish and exclusive."[2] That the term *anti–Semitism* had to wait until the mid–nineteenth century to be invented and that it arises out of a pseudoscientific proclamation such as this, of course, does not justify its exclusion from the Oxford English Dictionary, though indeed these things help to explain it. Its admission would be an admission.

The second answer to the riddle requires further clarification. If the term *anti–Semitism* did not come into being until the nineteenth century, should we conclude that no anti–Jewish bias existed prior to this time? Obviously not. But earlier forms of Jew hatred or prejudice were not based on racial theories. Rather, they originated in religious *anti–Judaism*, that is, in the theological–historical belief that not only were the Jews in general and in particular one eponymous Jew named Judas, responsible for the death of Christ, but throughout the long years following, they remained stiff–necked and unwilling to accept

83

the truth of Christ. Therefore, the reasoning went, Jews are nothing less than the devil's agents on earth, less than human opponents of Christian theology. As long as the Christian argument was universally espoused, almost all of Western literature—including English, as well as American literature, which was the child of English and European literature—was anti–Judaic in the sense that it represented the Jew as antagonist to the Christian scheme of salvation. The bias, then, arises out of Christian dogma.

In English literature we need only point to some of the greatest works of the Middle Ages and Renaissance. From the medieval period, we simply may recall the Mystery Play cycles, which include the texts of the Passion Plays. Or we can find folk myth anti–Judaism in "The Prioress's Tale" of Chaucer's *Canterbury Tales*, a story of blood libel. From the Renaissance, we only need summon Shakespeare's Shylock or Marlowe's Jew of Malta (aptly named Barabas, after the Jewish criminal who lived that Christ might die).

Of course, one correctly may point out that Barabas and Shylock are secular figures hated for their Machiavellian character, for their money lust and legalism. Yet such secular spin–offs of the Jew animus would not have been possible without the hard core of anti–Judaic propaganda that had begun in Christian Scripture and liturgy and had flowered in popular literature—in ballad, in drama, and in tale. Now add the psychological factor that once the Jew is established as absolute other—as archetypal antagonist to the Christian theological design—he automatically becomes the eternal evil opponent of everything people believe to be good. And people tend to come to terms with evil by disassociating themselves from it, that is, by projecting evil as demonic archetypal images or by seeing others as demonic. Thus, in a manner of speaking, these projections or archetypes are the scapegoats on which are placed either personal or communal ideas of evil.

Still, psychological archetypes hardly ever appear in a single, constant shape. Evil does not always manifest itself as a red devil with tail, arched eyebrows, cloven hoof, and pitchfork. More nearly, archetypes tend to be expressed in what some call a complex or complicated cluster of attitudes towards emotions such as being in love or, its opposite, having a phobia. As one wise person said, "Love blinds us to faults; hatred blinds us to virtues." These complexes can manifest themselves in a multiplicity of shapes. The erotic other can look like Helen of Troy or Annie Hall, but she is still the projection of erotic longing. So, in all religions, in all mythologies, in all our night dreams and daydreams, as in literature, the same archetypal figures occur over and over again. Only of that time or this place they wear different dress.

This explains the persistence of a fundamental mythic image, stereotype if you will, of the Jew in English literature and, at a certain historical point, in its descendent, American literature. The essentially demonic, evil, mythic projection of the Jew appears in literature from the New Testament characterization of Judas, the betrayer for money, on down to our own times, though that projection is given a local habitation and a name. Lionel Trilling put it simply: "The Jew in fiction was always an abstraction, a symbol, a racial stereotype created by men whose chief concern was obviously much less to tell the truth about the character of the Jew than it was to save their own political and economic interests and their own emotional needs." Trilling goes on to explain that the Jew in fiction is fundamentally a myth that "serves some purpose of explanation or projection for its makers." Hence, we can see that in the God–centered theological universe of the Middle Ages, the Jew functioned as an escape hatch for sin, guilt, and evil. In the Renaissance, an era of middle–class commercial aspiration and high politics, the Jew was an economic and political pressure valve. And as Trilling wrote in 1931, "the Jew is a political safety valve for Hitlerites."[3] The same could be said for Soviet stereotypes in our time and for portrayals of the third world as well. Only now the myth is contained no longer in the catch phrase *anti–Judaism* or *anti–Semitism*, but rather in its newest mutation, the geopolitical version, *Zionism*.

As the child of English literature, American writing fostered new figures on new soil based on the English collection of unforgettable Jewish fictional types. After all, by the time the New World began to be colonized (Plymouth being founded in 1620), the English literary imagination already had produced such enduring characters as Chaucer's Prioress, Marlowe's Jew of Malta, and Shakespeare's Shylock, not to mention the "Ballad of the Jew's Daughter," a popular song on the fashionable subject of ritual murder that comes down to us today in twenty–one versions, or those two malevolent Jewish physicians in what is commonly regarded as the first English historical novel, Thomas Nashe's *The Unfortunate Traveller*. Yet, where in American literature do we have such larger–than–life images of the Jew? Certainly in the colonial, revolutionary, and post–Federalist times, none comes to mind. And in the nineteenth century, can anything in our literature match the magnitude of Dickens's Fagin?

This observation might prompt the partially correct explanation that America, especially its literary center, New England, was founded as a haven for the human spirit by dissenting Puritans who brought with them to the New Zion ideals derived from zealous devotion to the Hebrew Bible. Having been persecuted themselves, they would not be likely to write with ill will towards the descendents of their beloved Hebrews. This, as we shall see, is only a partial explanation, for if such were the whole case, wouldn't we expect to find parallels to the great figures of nineteenth- and early twentieth–century English fiction who countered the mythic representation of the

Jew? Do we have a Rebecca of *Ivanhoe* fame? Where is our Daniel Deronda or Leopold Bloom?

Another explanation might be that we have not produced any writers of the genius of Chaucer, Shakespeare, Eliot, Dickens, or Joyce. Perhaps so, but even this does not sufficiently account for the absence, until the twentieth century, of great Jewish figures in American literature. After all, we had a Washington Irving who gave us Ichabod Crane and Rip Van Winkle. We had a James Fenimore Cooper who gave us Natty Bumppo. And by the mid–nineteenth century, we could list to our credit such permanent contributions to our collective consciousness as Hawthorne's Hester Prynne, Melville's Captain Ahab, Twain's Huck Finn, and the powerful images of Whitman and Poe. Why then is there no Jewish character, either negative or positive, of any magnitude? The answer is not a simple one and requires examination of a complex of factors.

Let us return for a moment to the Puritans. True, even in England, not surprisingly, Puritan writers did not produce anti–Judaic stereotypes. In fact, the seventeenth century, which was marked by the Puritan Cromwell's political revolution, was remarkable for the absence of the contemporary Jew from its literature. Instead, there emerged biblical Hebrew heroes of great power like Milton's Samson, for the Puritans were zealous readers of the Hebrew Bible and venerated the ancient heroes, seeing themselves and England as the great fulfillment of the Biblical promise. To use a contemporary analogy, they regarded England as the New Zion and the English as the new Israelites. This tradition was brought lock, stock, and barrel to America. Defeated in England, the Puritans looked to America even more as the new Promised Land. Such a deep conviction found eloquent expression in poet Timothy Dwight's epic on the American War for Independence, *The Conquest of Canaan*, in which Joshua represents George Washington.

But another curious fact must be noted: there were no Jews to speak of in England between 1292, when they had been expelled, and 1656, when Cromwell readmitted them. Still, as we have seen, the virtual absence of Jews did not prevent Chaucer, Marlowe, and Shakespeare from inventing them, for they could draw on a long history of Western anti–Jewish conventions, a history in which the only religious threat or outsider was the Jew. They had a full reservoir of stock figures upon which to draw. So although they did not have contemporary Jews on which to base their fictional characters, they had fifteen hundred years of religious tradition and folklore to provide them with readily recognizable types.

Quite to the contrary, there were *real* Jews in America almost from the start. In fact, by the end of the eighteenth century, records show almost three thousand Jews in the total population of roughly five million. This was not a very large proportion, to be sure, and these three thousand tended to live in cities, the largest Jewish communities being located in New York, Newport, Philadelphia, Lancaster (Pennsylvania), and Charleston (surprisingly the largest). But literary activity did not happen to be in the South, or even in Philadelphia or New York. It was centered in New England, where few Jews lived among the many Puritans, who continued to regard themselves as the logical fulfillment of God's promise to Israel. Moreover, the Puritans not only brought with them their veneration for the Hebrew hero, but they brought as well at least a surface commitment to biblical social idealism. In this American asylum for the oppressed, they expressed their democratic impulse towards egalitarianism. This, of course, is not to suggest that the colonial period was entirely free from religious prejudice. On the contrary, Protestant dissenters and Catholics fared badly, even more so than Jews. Undoubtedly this was because here the Jews were much less of a threat; hence, Quakers and Baptists became the ready scapegoats. And all the while slavery continued. Against the foreground of Protestant sects and black slaves, the Jews were certainly better off than they were any place else in the world, for at least in America they had the appearance of civil liberties. If this was the Promised Land for the Puritans, Jews who had long known the bitter taste of exile and persecution should have found it a comparative Eden.

Still, this does not tell the whole tale. Even if the Puritans revered the Hebrew Bible, other facets of the colonial spirit have to be mentioned. The middle colonies, for example, were less inspired by biblical ideals than they were by the spirit of enlightenment, by European egalitarian concerns for general toleration, civil liberties, and democratic government. Theirs was the new secular spirit and a new urban enterprise.

These men and women of the Age of Reason also held to the deistic religious belief in a God who rules the world by established laws, but they did not believe in the divinity of Christ or subscribe to the idea of biblical revelation. Consequently, in contrast to the Puritans who venerated the Bible, these rationalist deists vilified the ancient Hebrews, calling their religion the origin of Christian superstition. Certainly it was easier to denounce the ancient Hebrews than to attack the New Testament or living Christians. It would seem logical, then, to assume that the consequence of denouncing the Bible would be rampant anti–Judaism. In Europe such was precisely the case. Voltaire is the perfect example. In America, for reasons not hard to see, the spirit of enlightenment, democracy, toleration, and other such ideals worked against anti–Jewish attitudes.

Louis Harap points out in his comprehensive work, *The Imaqe of the Jew in American Literature,* that Thomas Jefferson denounced the ancient Jewish code in a letter to John Adams in 1813. "What a wretched depravity of sentiment and manners must have obtained before such corrupt maxims could have obtained credit," wrote Jefferson. But Harap goes on to tell us that "Adams, although an Enlightenment man in important respects, maintained a conservatism in his latter days permeated by the Calvinistic view of human nature, and consequently he had a more sympathetic view of the Biblical models revered by the Puritans. So in his reply to Jefferson he rose to the Jews' defense. 'The Hebrews,' he wrote, 'have done more to civilize man than any other nation.'"[4]

Add to this cluster of attitudes toward Jews the factor of continued Christian theological concern for them. This belief held that there would be no second coming of Christ until the conversion of the Jews. Undoubtedly, it is partially for this reason that the Jews have survived centuries of persecution. Logically speaking, if there are no Jews, how can there be a second coming? Towards this goal, then, the Puritan preacher Cotton Mather urged evangelizing any available Jews. The president of Yale, Ezra Stiles, well known for his amicable relationship with local Jews and visiting Rabbis, was moved to write in his diary of Jewish merchant Aaron Lopez (whose tombstone bears words by Stiles), "Oh! how often have I wished that sincere, pious, and candid man could have perceived the Evidences of Christianity, perceived the Truth as it is in Jesus Christ, known that *Jesus* was the *Messiah* predicted by Moses and the Prophets."[5] Hannah Adams, who wrote America's first history of the Jews and who was America's first professional woman writer, exhibited great admiration and sympathy for the Jews, yet was unable to comprehend Jewish refusal to accept Christian truth. "The history of the Jews exhibits a melancholy picture of human wretchedness and depravity," she wrote,

> On one hand we contemplate the lineal descendants of the chosen people of God, forfeiting their inestimable privileges by rejecting the glory of Israel, and involving themselves in the most terrible calamities; condemned to behold the destruction of their city and temple; expelled from their native country; dispersed through the world; by turns persecuted by Pagans, Christians and Moslems; continually duped by imposters, yet still persisting in rejecting the true Messiah.[6]

Thus, during the formative period of American history, we find conflicting positions regarding the ancient Hebrews and their descendants. Yet happily we can say that Jews were not projected in negative images in the literary works of the time. And, as we shall see, Jews do not play a significant part in American fiction for its first 150 years.

But, surprisingly, in a work by the first serious novelist in America, Charles Brockden Brown, a Jewish woman plays a central role. The hero of Brown's novel, *Arthur Mervyn* (published in 1799), is twenty years old and is about to recover his lost fortune by marrying a woman six years older than he. The Jewish woman, Achsa Fielding, came to America from England the year before the novel opens. We learn that when she was in England, she married an Englishman whose father consented to the marriage because he wanted his son to marry into money, but he required that the bride join the Anglican Church, which Achsa did. Achsa had no difficulty with this because, as she says, she was indifferent to religion and to the "disrepute and scorn to which the Jewish nation are everywhere condemned."[7] After this marriage, Achsa was plagued by a string of tragedies—her father committed suicide because of financial problems, her mother lost her mind, her child died, and her husband ran off with another woman. Recouping her fortune to go to America and begin life anew, Achsa ends her sad tale by happily marrying the hero of Brown's novel, Arthur Mervyn, who exhibits no strong anti–Jewish feelings, not even when he first discovers her Jewish background. He just registers a little surprise.

Even though this novel is virtually free from conventional stereotypes of Jews—the Jewish male as money lender, the social climber, the patriarchal legalist—it does hint at the old pattern of the Jewish daughter. Achsa, though not beautiful in the accepted sense of the word, is described as possessing mysterious eyes, manners of grace, the quickest and keenest penetration, and the power to bewitch. Indeed, she is but a variant of the archetypal Jewish woman as exotic erotic, and what keeps her "kosher" is her willingness to assimilate. She is first cousin to Abigail of Marlowe's *Jew of Malta* and Jessica of Shakespeare's *Merchant of Venice*, and in her mysterious sexuality she is close kin to Scott's Rebecca in *Ivanhoe*. As such, she is suitable for Arthur Mervyn to marry.

Although this fictional portrait of the Jewess appears early in the history of American literature, it does not immediately set the stage for much more of the same. In fact, as Louis Harap correctly observes, until the third decade of the nineteenth century, no further fully conceived Jewish characters are to be found, though from time to time one may run across the conventional cliches or references to Jewish stereotypes. After the 1830s, a sociological change began to occur in the American Jewish community that was bound to affect the literature. Until then the Jewish population, though Ashkenazic, was Sephardic in ritual. By 1830, thousands of German Jews began to flee to America, impelled by severe discriminatory conditions in Germany. The Jewish population swelled to enormous proportions after the revolution of 1848, increasing from three thousand to a hundred thousand in three decades. With this, the Jew became quite visible and an integral part of America's expanding economy. A change in attitude among non–Jews inevitably came about as a consequence of economic competition and social aspiration. Thus, by the middle of the nineteenth century, fictional depictions of and allusions to Jews

began to show up in quite unfavorable ways. Most often the stereotypes reappeared of the Jew as money lender or pawnbroker.

Perhaps the period's most curious invention was the amalgam of
the old–fashioned Jewish stereotype and the Gothic novel, which had
newly come to America, resulting in a home–designed product replete with violence, pornography, and the author's own brand of
populism. *Quaker City*, by George Lippard, was published as a book
in 1845, but it began its life a year earlier as a ten–part serial in the
Saturday Evening Post. The serial was called *The Monks of Monk's
Hall*, Monk's Hall being a brothel and the monks being the out-
wardly respectable gentlemen—business types and professionals—who
frequent the brothel to act out their fantasies and to satisfy their ap-
petites. George Lippard, a victim of a bank failure, was convinced
that the rich were all exploiters, cheaters, and manipulators, who
through their corruption made victims of the poor. Lippard devoted
his entire journalistic and literary career to the exposure of the im-
morality of the wealthy and powerful. An almost inevitable corollary
of such hatred and fear was Lippard's xenophobia and anti–Semitism.

Quaker City, which ran through thirty editions in four years, is
Gothic in the extreme, evoking the dark world of nightmare fright.
Harap describes it as a novel of "lushly decorated rooms, underground vaults, skeletons, death pits, ghost rooms and eerie lighting—
and simultaneously populated by the worst cast of grotesque human
images—hunchbacks, dwarfs, deaf and dumb blacks, fornicating cler-
gymen and greasy millionaires salivating and hyper–ventilating over
the prospect of initiating drugged young virgins into the world of
sex."[8] Included in this horrific rogues' gallery is the conventional figure of the beak–nosed Jewish forger, blatantly named Gabriel Von
Gelt, who speaks in Yiddish dialect. (This may be the earliest example of Yiddish dialect in English.) Moreover, as Leslie Fiedler has
suggested, Von Gelt is the literary ancestor of the fictional gangster,
Meyer Wolfsheim, of *The Great Gatsby*.[9]

All of this is in the service of the author's crackbrained socialism,
born of his hatred of the rich. Hence his call for labor to wage a class
war. Though the nineteenth–century fictional garb is economic and
political, Lippard unwittingly betrays its naked form. He tells us himself that his purpose is to lift the cover from the "whited
Sepulchre."[10] Lippard, the former theological student, expresses his
venom in a theological image, referring to the attack on the Pharisees
mentioned in the Bible (Matthew 23, 27). Lippard essentially views
the Jews as hypocrites, a point that underscores my earlier statement
that whatever chameleon change may take place in the representation of the Jew, under its color, a chameleon is always a lizard—a Jew
is always anti–Christ, the devil's agent on earth.

So far, as we have seen, American Literature appears to have produced no great and powerful images of the Jew—no Shylocks, no Fagins, no Isaacs, no Daniel Derondas—but only marginal negative figures. We have seen that as early as 1798, the Jewish female makes an appearance, and as we come to the works of classic American literature, we will see the Jew is present in a variation on the theme of the Jewess as a mysterious dark projection of sexual fantasy.

This is the case for Nathaniel Hawthorne, whose fictional works exclude references to contemporary Jews, except for Miriam in *The Marble Faun*, but whose diary entries reveal his prejudices and erotic thoughts. Hawthorne had little contact with American Jews, but he did come into contact with Jews in Europe. He writes in his European notebooks that he visited a synagogue in Rome and was repelled by it, and he enters a long description of a dinner he attended at the home of the lord mayor of London, who happened to be Jewish. Seated across from the brother and sister–in–law of the lord mayor, he was both repelled and fascinated, enough to write in detail the following account:

My eyes were mostly drawn to a young lady who sat nearly opposite me, across the table. She was, I suppose, dark, and yet not dark, but rather seemed to be of pure white marble, yet not white; but of the purest and finest complexion, (without a shade of color in it, yet anything but sallow or sickly) that I ever beheld. Her hair was a wonderful deep, raven black, black as night, black as death; not raven black, for that has a shiny gloss, and hers had not; but it was hair never to be painted, nor described—wonderful hair, Jewish hair. Her nose had a beautiful outline, though I could see that it was Jewish too; and that, and all her features, were so fine that sculpture seemed a despicable art beside her; and certainly my pen is good for nothing. If any likeness of her could be given, it must be by sculpture, not painting. She was slender, and youthful, but yet had a stately and cold, though soft and womanly grace; and, looking at her, I saw what were the wives of the old patriarchs, in their maiden or early married days—what Rachel was, when Jacob wooed her seven years,· and seven more—what Judith was; for, womanly as she looked, I doubt not she could have slain a man, in a good cause—what Bathsheba was; only she seemed to have no sin in her—perhaps what Eve was, though one could hardly think her weak enough to eat the apple. I should never have thought of touching her, nor desired to touch her; for, whether owing to distinctness of race, my sense that she was a Jewess, or whatever else, I felt a sort of repugnance, simultaneously with my perception that she was an admirable creature....

But, at the right hand of this miraculous Jewess, there sat
the very Jew of Jews; the distilled essence of all the Jews that
have been born since Jacob's time; he was Judas Iscariot; he
was the Wandering Jew; he was the worst, and at the same
time, the truest type of his race, and contained within himself, I have no doubt, every old prophet and every old
clothesman, that ever the tribes produced; and he must have
been circumcised as much as ten times over. I never beheld
anything so ugly and disagreeable, and preposterous, and
laughable, as the outline of his profile; it was so hideously
Jewish, and so cruel, and so keen; and he had such an im-
mense beard that you could see no trace of a mouth, until he
opened it to speak, or to eat his dinner,—and then, indeed,
you were aware of a cave, in this density of beard. And yet
his manners and aspect, in spite of all, were those of a man
of the world, and a gentleman. Well; it is as hard to give an
idea of this ugly Jew, as of the beautiful Jewess.... I rejoiced
exceedingly in this Shylock, this Iscariot; for the sight of him
justified me in the repugnance I have always felt towards his
race.[11]

The portrait of the dark lady is astonishingly revealing. It exposes
Hawthorne's ambivalent repulsion—and attraction—an almost classic
portrait of the Jungian archetypal anima. This image no doubt in-
forms the fictional Miriam in *The Marble Faun*—that half–Jewish
symbol of both rebellion and emancipation, the embodiment of hidden longings, and as Philip Rahv points out, "a temptress offering the
ascetic sons of the puritans the 'treasure trove of a great sin.'"[12] Rahv
calls her, as well as her three counterparts, Beatrice, Zenobia, and
Hester Prynne, the "Dark Lady of Salem."

Hawthorne's portrait of the lord mayor's brother has other implications. Although, as we have noted, Hawthorne did not actually create fictional Jewish types, he did write Gothic tales that gave him
opportunity for expressing the repulsion he felt towards the "Jew of
Jews." In his Gothic novels of terror and romanticism, Hawthorne
turns to the figure of the Wandering Jew, who had been seized upon
as the mythic villain par excellence by European and English novelists
of the romantic period fascinated by the strange, the supernatural,
the horrifying, and the demonic. For Hawthorne, the legend of the
Wandering Jew provided the opportunity to disguise his contempt for
the contemporary Jew and Jews of all times in the ubiquitous Mephis-
tophelean figure, typical of Hawthorne, who makes his most memora-
ble appearance in *Ethan Brand* as the devil in the shape of an old
German Jew.

If Hawthorne's attitudes towards Jews are consistent—that is,
consistently negative—the same cannot be said of Melville. In the
Melville corpus we find both myth and counter–myth. Melville, who

it seems had little contact with Jews for most of his life, did not include in his fiction any serious representation of Jews, except some marginal stereotypical characters such as the Jewish pawnbrokers in *Redburn*. By and large, Melville's interest is biblical. His novels use biblical figures allegorically, as images of spiritual truth. Moreover, Melville's lifelong interest in the Bible as a repository of wisdom ultimately impelled him to travel to Palestine to immerse himself in the land and culture of the Bible. The result of the trip is the long, philosophic narrative poem, *Clarel*, in which Melville includes six fully conceived Jewish types. These portraits are drawn with sympathy and understanding, and they represent not only a wide range of Jews—from an American family to a black Jew from India—but also personify Melville's personal uncertainties and quests. Of particular note is Melville's portrait of Ruth, the young American Jewess with whom the hero, Clarel, falls in love. In a way, Ruth is a less fully human figure than the others, more of an abstraction, a myth—very much in the tradition of Jessica, Rebecca, Ascha, and Miriam—insofar as she is clearly a projection of idealization and sensual imagining. In one version of this myth, the dark lady either converts or becomes assimilated (like Jessica, Ascha, and Miriam); in the other variety, if she is committed to her Judaism and will not convert, she either goes away (like Rebecca, who goes off to do social work in Spain), or she dies, which is the fate of Ruth in *Clarel*.

Melville, then, is unique with regard to the depiction of Jews in American literature in the nineteenth century, for he alone has treated a wide range of Jewish characters in an intelligent and sympathetic way. Nothing else compares in the American literature of the entire century (and its only English counterpart is George Eliot's *Daniel Deronda*). Much more predictably, we find in Henry James a patrician sensibility offended both by the German Jews, who in the late nineteenth century had begun to enter high society, and by those masses of Eastern European Jews beginning to pour into New York's Lower East Side. I might mention, however, that for all the noxiousness of James's anti-Semitism, it was less virulent than that of his friend and fellow Brahmin, Henry Adams, whose xenophobia was only exceeded by his prejudice against Jews. Adams, however, was not unique—his antagonism toward Jews was shared by most of his genteel friends. Adams includes in his famous 1880 novel, *Democracy*, a Jew too obviously named Hartbeest Schneidekoupon.

But James is more important in the history of American literary anti-Semitism, mainly because he had the more profound literary influence. One of James's major themes is the contrast of American sincere yet crude provincialism with European sophistication and decadence. On this teeter-totter, the Jew stands in the middle, able to weigh either side down. In Europe the Jew serves as intruder into the aesthetic and social province that was once reserved for the gen-

teel elite. In America the Jew is portrayed as a less–than–human pol-
lutant adding to the general vulgarity. James's 1903 novel, *The Ambassadors*, describes the inelegant crowd that congregated in the stu-
dio of an artist named Gloriani: "Oh, they're everyone—all sorts and
sizes; of course, I mean within limits, though limits down, rather than
up. There are always artists...and then *gros bonnets* of many kinds—
ambassadors, cabinet ministers, bankers, generals, what do I know?
even Jews."[13] So much for the aggressive European Jew trying to
hobnob with what he thought was uppercrust.

In America, after making a visit to the old East Side in 1904,
James wrote about the "swarming" Jews of New York and reported
that "with the exception of some shy corner of Asia, no district in the
world known to the statistician has so many inhabitants to the yard."
The sights and smells offended his upper–class nose, and he was re-
minded of "small strange animals, known to natural history, snakes
or worms, I believe, who when cut in pieces, wriggle away and live in
the snippet as completely as in the whole." Of the East Side cafes, he
observed that they were "torture rooms of the living idiom," and he
"feared for the future of the English language."[14]

This fear was not to end with James. In a note to *The World of
Our Fathers*, Irving Howe tells us that "Katherine Anne Porter,
though not mentioning any individual writers, has attacked a curious
kind of argot, more or less originating in New York, a deadly mixture
of academic, guttersnipe, gangster, fake–Yiddish, and dull worn out
dirty words—an appalling bankruptcy in language, as if [these writers]
hate English and are trying to destroy it." Less charitably, Gore Vidal
has complained that "with each generation American prose grows
worse, reflecting confused thinking, poor education, and.the incomplete assimilation of immigrant English into the old language."[15]

At this point in the story of anti–Semitism in American literature,
we can observe an interesting pattern that calls to mind critic Philip
Rahv's famous essay on American literature, "Paleface and
Redskin." Rahv says that

> viewed historically American writers appear to group them-
> selves around two polar types. Paleface and redskin...and de-
> spite occasional efforts at reconciliation, no love is lost be-
> tween them. At one pole there is the literature of the lowlife
> of the frontier and of the big cities; at the other the thin,
> solemn, semi–clerical culture of Boston and Concord....So-
> ciologically the two types can be distinguished as patrician
> and plebian, and in their aesthetic ideals one is drawn to
> allegory and the distillations of symbolism, whereas the other
> inclines to a gross, riotous naturalism.[16]

As nineteenth–century examples of this polarity, Rahv cites palefaces
Hawthorne and James and redskins Twain and Whitman. Curiously,
until the twentieth century, the redskins are virtually innocent of

anti–Jewish bias in their writings, whereas the palefaces have been generous contributors to literary anti–Semitism. But this distinction holds only up to a point. Once the dominant palefaces were over- thrown in the twentieth century by the redskins, the score evened up.

True, the palefaces continued in their phobic attitudes towards Jews. Edith Wharton was guilty of this, T.S. Eliot even more so. Eliot, also a self–styled, patrician, American exile to England, was just as repelled as was James by the double intrusion of Jews into the American and the European culture. Eliot regarded the Jew as cor- rupter of the Western world at large. His blatant anti–Semitism has been a source of embarrassment to the literary establishment (as is Pound's). Much as many of Eliot's admirers would like to rescue him from charges of anti–Semitism, it is quite impossible to ignore such poems as "Burbank with Bedeker: Bleistein with Cigar" and "Geron- tion." Here the Jew is centrally positioned in Eliot's vision of the decay of Western civilization, a vision given its ultimate expression in *The Wasteland*, that long expression of the poet's despair about the decay and disintegration of European Christian culture. Eliot puts it this way in "Gerontion," where the word *house* stands for Western culture:

My house is a decayed house,
And the Jew squats on the window sill, the owner
Spawned in some estaminet of Antwerp,
Blistered in Brussels, patched and peeled in London.[17]

While Edith Wharton, T.S. Eliot, F. Scott Fitzgerald, and other palefaces continued in their genteel biases, something new was hap- pening on the American literary scene. Leslie Fiedler points out that in the earlier decades of this century, provincial writers such as Sher- wood Anderson and Sinclair Lewis (of *Winesburg, Ohio* and *Main Street* fame) were really an extension of the "long term Anglo–Saxon domination of our literature." But in the generation just before World War I, a shift away from the provinces began to occur, and the urban novel began its career. This urbanization of the novel, in fact, al- lowed the American Jewish novelist to begin to play a critical role in the development of American literature. This is true, Fiedler tells us, because the subject of the Jewish novelist, Jewish ghetto life, was urban. Moreover, evidence that the palefaces were losing their hold and the redskins were on the upward move was signaled by the emer- gence of Theodore Dreiser as the first novelist of immigrant stock to claim a major position in American fiction. "There is something ironic," Fiedler goes on to say, "in the fact that the break through which succeeding Jewish writers poured was opened by one not inno- cent of anti–Semitism."[18] Fiedler's understatement can be summed up in Dreiser's comment to his mentor, the notoriously anti–Semitic H.L. Mencken. Dreiser wrote a letter to Mencken in 1922 in which he explodes, "N.Y. to me is a scream—A Kyke's dream of a Ghetto. The lost tribe has taken the island."[19]

Conventional attitudes similar to these began to appear everywhere in American fiction and poetry—in the work of paleface and redskin alike—as the Jew became the symbol of the rich capitalist, the poor communist, the defender of blacks, the detractor of blacks, the vulgar social climber, the pushy intellectual, all things to all people—"more devils than vast hell can hold."[20] The mythic image of the Jew, male and female, can be found in its infinite variety in Thomas Wolfe, William Faulkner, Ezra Pound, John Updike, William Styron, and too many others to name. Perhaps one more variety now should not go unmentioned—that is, the anti-Zionist version of Jewish myth perhaps present in submerged form in John Le Carre's *Little Drummer Girl* and presented openly in the Costa-Gavros film *Hannah K.*

Of course, during these years, the American-Jewish novelist added to the stock of fictional images of the Jew. Obviously, I cannot deal with such an enormous topic in this essay, but I would like to make three short observations. First, for a long time the Jewish writer appeared to have swallowed whole the Gentile myth, only to regurgitate it in sour self-hatred. Consider, for example, Ben Hecht's *A Jew in Love* or Philip Roth's *Portnoy's Complaint*. Otherwise, the Jewish writer seized upon the counter-myth of George Eliot's *Daniel Deronda*, the myth of the mystique of the assimilated Jew who sets out on a quest of rediscovery. This appears in Ludwig Lewissohn's *The Island Within*. The Jewish writer also adopted James Joyce's version, in Leopold Bloom, of the Jew as metaphor for everyman as outsider. Bernard Malamud does this in *The Assistant*, as does Robert Greenfield in *Temple*. Second, American Jewish fiction has run the course from accommodation to assimilation to affirmation, from Abraham Cahan's *Yekl: A Tale of the New York Ghetto* and *The Rise of David Levinsky*, through Jerome Weidman's *What Makes Sammy Run* and Bruce Jay Friedman's *A Mother's Kisses,* to Saul Bellow's *Herzog* and virtually all of the fiction of Cynthia Ozick. Third, the very prominence of the American-Jewish writer dressed the myth in a new costume in the second half of the twentieth century. This guise appears in John Updike's *Bech: A Book* and *Bech Is Back* and as the competitor against which William Styron's Stingo is running his literary race in *Sophie's Choice*. Whether we shall be able to eliminate anti-Semitic images from American literature in what is left of this century, or whether they simply will take on new forms related to our preoccupations with high technology and our space-age manias, remains to be seen.

Notes

1. Lucy S. Dawidowicz, *The War against the Jews* (New York: Holt, Rinehart and Winston, 1975), p. 43.

2. Quoted in Dawidowicz, p. 41.

3. Lionel Trilling, "The Changing Myth of the Jew," *Commentary*, August 1978, p. 25.

4. Louis Harap, *The Image of the Jew in American Literature* (Philadelphia: The Jewish Publication Society, 1974), p. 24. It is interesting to note that Adams identified the Hebrews as a nation, not a race.

5. Ibid., p. 26.

6. Ibid., p. 27.

7. Charles Brockden Brown, *Arthur Mervyn: Or Memoirs of the Year 1783* (New York: Holt, Rinehart and Winston, 1962), p. 417.

8. Harap, *The Jew in American Literature*, p. 48.

9. Leslie Fiedler, "The Jew in the American Novel," in *The Collected Essays of Leslie Fiedler*, vol. 2 (New York: Stein and Day, 1971), p. 68.

10. George Lippard, *The Empire City; or New York by Night and Day, Its Aristocracy and Its Dollars* (Philadelphia: P.B. Peterson and Bros., 1864), p. 205.

11. Nathaniel Hawthorne, *The English Notebooks*, ed. Randall Stewart (New York: Modern Language Association of America, 1941), p. 321.

12. Philip Rahv, "The Dark Lady of Salem," in *Image and Idea* (Connecticut: New Directions, 1957), p. 33.

13. Henry James, *The Ambassadors* (New York: Harper and Row, 1902), p. 137.

14. Henry James, quoted in Harap, *The Jew in American Literature*, p. 376.

15. Irving Howe, *The World of Our Fathers* (New York: Harcourt, Brace, Jovanovich, 1976), note 588.

16. Philip Rahv, "Paleface and Redskin," in *Image and Idea*, p. 1.

17. T.S. Eliot, "Gerontion," in *Collected Poems* (New York: Harcourt, Brace and World, 1934), p. 29, lines 7-10.

18. Fiedler, "The Jew in the American Novel," p. 85.

19. Theodore Dreiser, *The Letters of Theodore Dreiser*, vol. 2, Robert H. Elias, ed. (Philadelphia: University of Pennsylvania Press, 1959), p. 405.

20. William Shakespeare, *A Midsummer Night's Dream*, act 5, scene 1, line 9.

Chapter 6

Shakespeare's Shylock and Ours

Nicholas A. Sharp

Sometimes, a writer, a philosopher, or a politician will seize upon a work of art, reinterpret it, and use it to support some new or radical idea. Hitler did it with the Ring Cycle.[1] Freud did it with *Oedipus Rex*.[2] They both did it so well that today we can hardly believe that Wagner was not a Nazi, Sophocles not a psychoanalyst. Shakespeare, too, has often been dragged into ideological conflicts. In the 1940s Paul Robeson helped make *Othello* a subject for racial controversy. In the 1930s, Orson Welles used his Brown Shirt version of *Julius Caesar* to make Shakespeare an antifascist.[3] *The Tempest* has often been rerendered as a plea for humane values in an industrial–technological era.[4]

There's nothing inherently wrong with such adaptations. To the contrary, they help keep the traditional masterpieces vital. I may disagree profoundly with Germaine Greer's feminist revisions of Marlowe and Bacon in *The Female Eunuch*, but I honor her for recognizing their importance.[5]

The problem that can arise from such reinterpretations of art, however, is that they can settle so deeply into our consciousness that we lose the power to distinguish between the contemporary uses of the work and the work itself. I knew a man who couldn't listen to Wagner because all he could hear was a paean to the ideals of the Third Reich. I once watched a fine, sensitive production of *Hamlet* with a psychiatric social worker who could see nothing in the tragedy except an illustration of Freudian psychology. In both cases, the problem was not that the people were wrong in their interpretations, but rather that they were so locked into a single, ideological viewpoint that they had lost the power to recognize other, perhaps equally powerful, possibilities in the work, possibilities that might have been truly valuable to them.

Shakespeare's Shylock, the "tragic villain" (if I may be excused such a neologism) of *The Merchant of Venice* may be the best example I could cite for the ways that people confuse current reinterpretations of a work with the work itself. The figure of Shylock has become so thoroughly enmeshed with modern notions of anti–Semitism and anti–anti–Semitism that audiences, critics, actors, and directors frequently lose their power to see the work clearly for what it is. They also lose the power to learn some things that the play might otherwise be able to show them.

It seems worthwhile, therefore, to spend a little time trying to distinguish between Shakespeare's Shylock and our own, not only as a way of opening our minds to the possibilities in that one great character, but also as an exercise in learning (or perhaps improving) our general ability to approach and interpret art with the kind of openness that real creative work (as distinguished from propaganda) should inspire.

Let me make it clear at the outset, then, that I believe any approach to *The Merchant of Venice* that portrays Shylock as a tragically heroic victim of bigotry and prejudice imposes modern perspectives on the play. Shylock is, of course, a victim. Shakespeare makes it clear that Antonio (at least) has bullied and humiliated Shylock publically. Antonio, says Shylock, has publically assailed him as "misbeliever, cut–throat dog, and spet upon my Jewish gaberdine" (act 1, scene 3, lines 111–112).[6] Antonio's answer is "I am as like to call thee so again, to spet on thee again" (act 1, scene 3, lines 130–131). Later Shylock says the reason for such treatment is simply that "I am a Jew" (act 3, scene 1, line 58). No audience can ever doubt that Shylock has been victimized by prejudice and bigotry.

Shylock is not, however, a hero, and to call him tragic is wrong. In the first place, the form of the play denies that he can be a hero. He speaks mostly prose, for instance, hardly any verse. Moreover, Shylock is the obstructing father of a beautiful young lover, Jessica. Since Roman times, such characters have never been heroic.[7] Certainly in Shakespeare's plays they never are. Think of old Montague and old Capulet in *Romeo and Juliet* or of the real and the usurping Dukes in *As You Like It*. Fathers who interfere with their children's love affairs can be solemn, pathetic, sad, or funny, but not heroic. And if we make Shylock's final moments on the stage a tragedy, then we are left with half of one act and all of another to explain.

No. Although since Henry Irving's tragic Shylock (in 1879) or even since Edmund Kean's pathetic Shylock (in 1814),[8] this character has steadily grown more and more appealing in the minds and hearts of audiences, we err today when we see him as the center of the play, a hero in a tragedy about the Jew of Venice rather than the villain of a romantic comedy called *The Merchant of Venice*. As created and originally presented by Shakespeare and his theatrical company in the late 1590s, Shylock was a villain, a wicked and wrongheaded man whose Jewish identity and faith were portrayed as contributing to his unjust and cruel intents.[9]

With that understood, however, let me quickly add that the most astonishing fact about this ugly and bigoted portrait of the Jew is its human and humane treatment, despite its strong anti–Semitic odor. Shylock as conceived by Shakespeare was an anti–Semitic caricature, yet even in creating this distorted cartoon of Jewishness, Shakespeare simultaneously gave his character the one crucial element that the worst of anti–Semites would deny—humanity. Shylock is evil, but he is human. He is wicked, but he is neither a beast nor a devil. He is a man. In the context of the times, the creation of a Jewish villain who yet retains the essential dignity of his humanity was nothing short of wonderful, especially in a play created for a mass audience composed almost exclusively of rabid anti–Semites.

Remember, Elizabethan England had more thoroughly institutionalized its anti–Semitism than had almost any other country in Europe.[10] There never was a large Jewish population in England, but in 1290 Edward I banished those few who were there. Unlike countries that restricted Jewish rights, England simply said, no Jews allowed—on penalty of death. For centuries—until 1655—they kept that policy. To set foot in fourteenth–, fifteenth–, or sixteenth–century England and live, a Jew had to conceal his identity, deny his faith, and obtain special permission from a fickle and suspicious monarch who might on any whim withdraw that permission and impose the penalty demanded by law.

Few Jews chose to visit England, and without any real, live Jewish human beings to contradict their fantasies, Englishmen developed a host of anti–Semitic beliefs. Chaucer, for instance, the most popular poet of pre–Shakespearean England, wrote "The Prioress's Tale" about a Jewish ritual murder of a pious Christian orphan, and his story was widely believed to be true.[11] Preachers and pamphleteers, bishops and ballad–mongers manufactured the most bizarre allegations about Jewish doctrines and beliefs, Jewish dietary and sexual practices, completely without fear of contradiction. Of course, in sixteenth–century England, Protestants and Catholics, Presbyterians and Episcopalians, monarchists and parliamentarians regularly accused each other of the most remarkable aberrations (Jesuits were said to be trained assassins, and Puritans were accused of sodomy), but all could agree that the worst degeneracies were practiced by those who denied even the name of Christ, the Jews.[12]

Not surprisingly, therefore, the most popular and successful Elizabethan literature about Jews had an almost surrealistic element of sadism and depravity. During the decade before Shakespeare's *Merchant*, Marlowe's *The Jew of Malta* was a successful and popular play. Marlowe's Barabas is a tissue of horrors—he poisons a convent of nuns who have harbored his daughter, for instance—but he is no more human or credible than the Dracula of modern mythology. Similarly, the character of Abraham, the professional poisoner who masquerades as a physician in Robert Green's successful play, *The Tragicall Raigne of Selimus, Emperor of the Turks* (1594), is delighted to commit any crime for money. And Thomas Nashe's extremely successful prose narrative, *The Unfortunate Traveller* (1594), includes the unbelievably depraved character of Zakok, a truly monstrous creation. He specializes in the flagellation of Christian women. Then, besides selling the main character into slavery (to another Jew, who wants to use him for medical experiments), he speculates about the pleasures of poisoning the water supply of Rome or contaminating the city's bread and watching the entire population die. Nashe eventually has Zakok caught and enthusiastically describes the villain's torture and death. Such was the Elizabethan literary image of Jews.

Moreover, in 1594 one of the few Jews courageous enough to attempt a life in England, the Portuguese convert Roderigo Lopez, personal physician to Elizabeth I, was accused, tried, and convicted of conspiring with the Spanish to poison the queen by rubbing poison on the pommel of her saddle. Prosecuted by Shakespeare's patron, the Earl of Essex, and convicted without proof of anything except being a Jew, Lopez was vilified in the most lurid kinds of popular literature and was hanged, drawn, and quartered before a huge crowd of jeering and angry Londoners.[13]

Three years later, Shakespeare's *Merchant* went on the boards. In such an environment, Shakespeare's portrayal of Shylock seems almost incredibly positive. Indeed, his whole portrayal of Jews seems surprisingly warm, for with the exception of Shylock, the Jewish figures of the drama are very attractive. Tubal, Shylock's friend, has a very minor role, but he performs his function gravely and with dignity. Jessica, Shylock's daughter, comes across as a vain and thoughtless young girl, but charming and attractive—a sort of Venetian Juliet, guilty of nothing save a romantic attachment to a man her father cannot accept and a willingness to defy parental authority.

Shylock, on the other hand, is unrelentingly a villain. He mentions his Jewishness again and again, and he makes the most damning statements about his faith and race. Of Antonio, Shylock says, "I hate him for he is a Christian" (act 1, scene 3, line 42), marking himself as the product of an anti–Semitic bigot's imagination. He defends usury (still widely held to be a sin in the Elizabethan mind) by quoting precedent from Genesis, and he is reviled with "the devil can cite Scripture" (act 1, scene 2, line 98). He refuses to eat with Christians, and he worries incessantly about money and revenge. Shylock is a thorough burlesque of Judaism, a cruel parody produced by ignorance, superstition, and prejudice.

And yet, though his Jewishness is rendered maliciously, Shylock's humanity is presented sympathetically and with a care to reveal valid motives for his hatred and the grievances behind his lust for revenge. Shylock may hate Antonio for being a Christian, but he hates the Venetian even more for some very human reasons, too. Antonio has been an active and, by Shylock's standards, an unfair business competitor. Far worse, he has also been an aggressive anti–Semite who rails against all Jews and curses them in public. He has even spit upon Shylock and humiliated him repeatedly.

When Jessica leaves home and begins to spend the money she has stolen from her father, Shylock is reported to have bemoaned his wealth, but he also grieves the loss of his daughter. "My daughter! 0 my ducats! 0 my daughter!" (act 2, scene 8, line 15) is surely a set of shared emotions that anyone, Jew or Gentile, can imagine in Shylock's situation, especially since one of the stolen stones was a ring given Shylock by his wife, who is now dead.

Most importantly, Shakespeare gave Shylock one of the great dramatic speeches of all English literatue, the famous "I am a Jew. Hath not a Jew eyes?" speech of act 3, scene 1. Shylock takes center stage and, even in a production presenting him unsympathetically, he wins from the audience a recognition that he is, faults and all, a human being with human feelings and a human heart. A Jew, he argues, may do evil things, but he is human. Jews are not different from Christians in their need to have their essential human dignity respected. In all of written English, this is the single most persuasive passage in defense of toleration. It is the most potent argument ever mounted for a recognition that Jews, too, have the same human rights as Christians, no matter what their civil or legal or religious rights may be.

Shakespeare's Shylock, in other words, is no tragic hero. His forced conversion at the end of act 4 is intended as an act of mercy, for he clearly deserves to die. Moreover, his villainy is portrayed as an inescapable part of his religious and ethnic identity as a Jew. He was created by an anti–Semite, and he expresses and promotes a set of bigoted, ignorant, and stupid prejudices against Jews. At the same time, he is one of the earliest—still the greatest—English portrayals of a Jew as a human being, a person with feelings, sensitivities, and above all, a native dignity that he shares with all other human beings—Christian, Muslim, pagan, or Jew.

In the context of the times, this accomplishment is simply extraordinary. A victim of the ignorance and superstition of his age (who has ever escaped the influences of such?), Shakespeare yet created a villain whose humanity could be felt and recognized by audiences of all times. His Shylock was not, perhaps, the noble and pathetic figure promoted by Kean and Irving in the nineteenth century, nor was he the intelligent, tragic figure of George C. Scott's masterfully modern portrayal.[14] But he was and is human.

When all is said and done, that is the insight from which all arguments against anti–Semitism must begin. It is the one seed from which all forms of pluralistic civility and mutual respect must grow. It is the one thing, in Shakespeare's Shylock and, one hopes, in ours of the twentieth century, that elevates this play and this character to a level that transcends the moment or the decade, the one thing that keeps him alive for the ages.

Notes

1. According to Geoffrey Skelton's *Wagner at Bayreuth: Experiment and Tradition* (London: Barrie and Rockliff, 1965), the fact that "Hitler enjoyed his Wagner in splendid array and was prepared to pay for it" (p. 152) is one reason why Heinz Tietjen's sumptuously spectacular, Nazi–controlled productions at Bayreuth from 1933 to 1939 still define Wagner for many people. According to Skelton, the Nazis even asked Tietjen to paint swastikas on the shields of the Gibichungs in *Gotterdammerung*, though he refused.

2. See especially Sigmund Freud, *The Interpretation of Dreams*, trans. James Strachey (New York: Basic Books, 1955), pp. 261–264.

3. See Bernard Grebanier, *Then Came Each Actor: Shakespearean Actors, Great and Otherwise, Including Players and Princes, Rogues, Vagabonds, and Actors Motley, from Will Kempe to Olivier and Gielgud and After* (New York: David McKay, 1985), pp. 463–464 (on Robeson's 1943 Othello as a "social conscience" issue) and p. 511 (on Welles's 1937 *Julius Caesar* and its "intelligent and undistorted parallel between Caesar and Mussolini").

4. For example, Paul Mazursky's 1983 Columbia film, *Tempest*, with John Cassavetes as Philip/Prospero.

5. Germaine Greer makes many references to medieval, Renaissance, and modern literature throughout *The Female Eunuch* (New York: McGraw–Hill, 1971).

6. References to *The Merchant of Venice* are from G. Blakemore Evans ed., *The Riverside Shakespeare* (Boston: Houghton–Mifflin, 1974).

7. See Northrop Frye, *Anatomy of Criticism: Four Essays* (Princeton, N.J.: Princeton University Press, 1957), pp. 163–186, especially pp. 164–165 on fathers as obstacles in comedy.

8. See Bernard Grebanier, *The Truth about Shylock* (New York: Random House, 1962), especially Chapter 9, "Other Men's Shylock," pp. 313–350. Henry Irving's great, tragic Shylock is summarized on pp. 332–334, and Edmund Kean's virile and pathetic Shylock is treated on pp. 328–329.

9. The most extreme modern proponent of Shylock as a villain was Elmer Edgar Stoll, whose "Shylock" first appeared in *The Journal of English and Germanic Philology* 10 (1911): 236–279, and was later reprinted in Stoll's *Shakespeare Studies* of 1927. Stoll brought forth massive historical evidence to support his vision of Shylock as a comic butt and of Shakespeare as an Elizabethan anti–Semite.

10. Grebanier, *Shylock*, Chapter 2, "Prick Them and They Do Not Bleed: Englishmen and the Jews," pp. 17–75, nicely summarizes

the legal and social history of both English Jews and English anti-Semitism.

11. See Grebanier, *Shylock*, pp. 17–75.

12. During the Tudor–Stuart period, English writers, lawyers, and orators raised slander, libel, invective, and satire to a fine art. See, for example, the description (by John Webster?) of "a Precision" and "a Jesuit" in the section on "The Overburian Character" in Herschel Baker ed., *The Later Renaissance in England: Nondramatic Verse and Prose, 1600–1660* (Boston: Houghton–Mifflin, 1975), p. 718.

13. For a brief, thorough summary, see the entry on Lopez in Oscar James Campbell and Edward G. Quinn, eds., *The Reader's Encyclopedia of Shakespeare* (New York: Crowell, 1966), p. 467.

14. Reviewing Joseph Papp's 1962 production of *The Merchant* in Central Park, *New York Times* reviewer Arthur Gelb called George C. Scott's Shylock "perfectly balanced—a multi-dimensional human being." See "Shakespeare Festival in Central Park," *The New York Times Theater Reviews*, June 22, 1962.

IV

Hopeful Conclusions

This last section explores relationships between Jews and Christians and between Jews and blacks.

The relationship between blacks and Jews, according to Weisbord and Kazarian, in Chapter 7, "'That Marvellous Movement': Early Black Views of Zionism," was influenced not so much by theological tension as it was by the ability of many black leaders to identify with the plight of Jews in Europe and with Jewish ethnic consciousness, suggesting "paradigms for transplanted Africans in the Americas." There is a remarkable history of pro-Zionist thought among black notables such as Edward Blyden, Booker T. Washington, W.E.B. Du Bois, Marcus Garvey, and Ralph Bunche. Weisbord and Kazarian explore the ideas of each of these leaders in terms of their attitudes toward the attempt to create a haven of refuge for persecuted Jews. Although these leaders differ in significant ways, a thread of agreement runs through their writings. Weisbord and Kazarian sum it up in the idea that "Zionism's chief value was as a model for victimized Diaspora blacks to copy." Zionism offered blacks "a constructive lesson in self-help." Even though Booker T. Washington differed from the others in terms of his willingness to accommodate, he still believed, as the authors quote him, that the "Negro has much to learn from the Jew."

This marvelous story is developed in detail in Weisbord's and Kazarian's fascinating book, published in 1985 by Greenwood Press, *Israel in the Black American Perspective*. With Weisbord's 1970 work (with Arthur Stein), *Bittersweet Encounter*, also put out by Greenwood Press, this book places Weisbord in the forefront of scholars who have studied the relationships between Jews and blacks. As he notes in these works, in recent years the relationship has turned from the early manifestation of black support for Zionism to a mixed relationship with expressions of contemporary hostility.

The concern with black anti-Semitism, however, cannot be seen in a vacuum. As both books point out, concern with black anti-Semitism in America has been a recurring theme for Jews and is one aspect of a complex relationship between the two groups.

To understand it, one must fit this relationship into the structural context of the United States and note that blacks and Jews are subjected to the same psychological, political, economic, and cultural influences that shape everyone's perceptions. This brief summary is not the place to highlight the history of relations between blacks and Jews, but it is necessary to point out that the 1980s are a particularly turbulent period. Anyone wishing to understand the contemporary situation should consult the two books mentioned above.

The relationship between Jews and Christians is addressed by Spiro in a final chapter on "Judaism and Christianity: Sources of Convergence." Jewish–Christian conflicts primarily are based on theological differences. Christians accuse Jews of rejecting their sacred beliefs, and Jews accuse Christians of injecting false beliefs into the authentic Judaism of the time of Jesus. Spiro points out that the basis of conflict and misunderstanding lies in literalist interpretations. Both Christian and Jewish theologies attempt to discover and relate to the infinite. The conflicts could be lessened if both traditions could admit that finite man cannot comprehend the infinite. Whatever we mean by "revelation," all our responses to hearing the divine voice are profoundly influenced by our human limitations. Thus, a key to mutual understanding and the abatement of tension requires accepting the fact that theological concepts—the revelation at Sinai, the Crucifixion, Torah, God—are metaphorical and not all–encompassing truth or ultimate reality. The metaphorical approach to theology teaches that all traditions fall short of the ultimate.

So do all collections of essays, the present one included. Yet we would like to conclude on a hopeful note and can do so by paraphrasing from Weisbord's and Kazarian's recent book. They conclude *Israel in the Black American Perspective* by pointing out that blacks and Jews share common interests in shaping a more just and equitable society. We would like to amplify this eloquent conclusion by broadening it to include all people. We would like it to read:

> [We must] share a fundamental vision of a just society devoid of racial or religious hatred....[The] common enemy [is] the bigot in whom anti–Semitism and [other racial or religious hatred] are integral elements....[All people] who forget this do so at their peril. (p. 184)

Chapter 7

"That Marvellous Movement": Early Black Views of Zionism

Robert Weisbord and Richard Kazarian, Jr.

After the conclusion of the American Civil War, which brought political freedom to approximately four million bondsmen, most blacks in the street—or more commonly on the plantation—had very little time to contemplate foreign affairs. Whether they lived in the North or the South, they were too preoccupied with physical and emotional survival for themselves and their families in a hostile and racially prejudiced environment. Reparations in the form of forty acres and a mule for each ex–slave had been proposed but never delivered. Consequently, acquiring even the most basic necessities of life was a formidable, all–consuming task.

Yet a few black intellectuals and leaders were well aware of developments overseas in Africa, Europe, and the Middle East, and some commented on obscure movements with what seemed to be only tenuous connections with the pressing realities of black Americans. Zionism, which aimed to establish a homeland for dispersed Jews in Palestine, their ancient homeland from which most had been expelled almost two millennia before, was one such movement. Jews drew the attention of some black thinkers who had been raised on the Old Testament and who saw a parallel between the enslavement and continuing travail of the "chosen people" and their own tragic history of thralldom and oppression. For some other blacks, the durable Jewish ethnic consciousness and Zionism's repatriationist answer to the question of survival suggested paradigms for transplanted Africans in the Americas.

One nineteenth–century black luminary, Edward Wilmot Blyden, fit into both categories. Born in St. Thomas, Virgin Islands, in 1832, Blyden enjoyed a remarkable multifaceted career. He was a true *uomo universale*, a Renaissance man. Blyden, who emigrated to

This chapter is based on Robert G. Weisbord, "The Marvellous Movement: Early Black Views of Zionism" in Robert Weisbord and Richard Kazarian, Jr., *Israel in the Black American Perspective* (Westport, Conn.: Greenwood Press, 1985), pp. 7–28. Copyright ©1985 by Robert G. Weisbord and Richard Kazarian, Jr. Used by permission of the publisher.

West Africa in 1851, was an editor, a prodigious writer of books and pamphlets, an extraordinary linguist, a professor of classics, Secretary of State of the newly established republic of Liberia, Liberian Ambassador to the Court of St. James, and President of Liberia College. In addition, he was a Pan–Negro patriot and an apostle of Diasporan black repatriation to Africa. In the informed opinion of his biographer, Hollis Lynch, he was "easily the most learned and articulate champion of Africa and the Negro race in his own time."[1]

Blyden's curiosity about and attraction to Jews was at least partly traceable to his boyhood in Danish St. Thomas, where a majority of the white population was Jewish. There he became familiar with Jewish festivals and traditions. There also he was first exposed to the Hebrew tongue. One of young Blyden's most ardent desires was to master Hebrew so that he could read the Old Testament and the Talmud in that ancient language.[2]

In 1866 Blyden spent three months visiting Lebanon, Syria, and Palestine. Peripatetic by nature, he had developed a yearning to travel to "the original home of the Jews—to see Jerusalem and Mt. Zion, the joy of the whole earth."[3] He was deeply moved by his initial glimpse of Jerusalem and was particularly touched by the Western Wall, the holiest Jewish site in that holy city.

The sizeable Jewish population then residing in Jerusalem, and which had done so for centuries, was clearly a religious community bereft of political aspirations. At that period in history, political Zionism was only embryonic in form and was fated to be stillborn.[4] In 1862, four years before Blyden's journey, Rabbi Zvi Hirsch Kalischer, who lived under Prussian rule, had published a book entitled *Derishat Zion (Seeking Zion)*. Truly a classic in Zionist literature, it meticulously outlined a program that would facilitate the purchase of villages, fields, and vineyards in the land of the Bible. Kalischer also envisioned the organization of self–defense units to protect colonists from hostile Bedouins and the creation of an agricultural school to teach inexperienced Jewish youth the skills of farming.[5]

The same year, Moses Hess, another pioneer Zionist, expounded his theory of Jewish nationalism in *Rome and Jerusalem*, which was also destined to become a fundamental document in Zionist annals.[6] Influenced by the various nationalist movements sweeping across Europe and stung by the persistence of anti–Semitism, Hess saw the Jewish future bound up with Palestine and became convinced that the political rebirth of the Jewish nation would be precipitated by the founding of Jewish colonies there. But the cries of the proto–Zionists, Kalischer and Hess, fell on deaf ears. European Jews pinned their hopes either on assimilation as a panacea or on an age–old messianic dream of divine redemption. As a general rule, Jews who travelled to Palestine in the nineteenth century went there to die, to be interred in holy soil rather than to live and build a Jewish nation.

In point of fact, Blyden in the 1860s and 1870s was much more of a Zionist than were most Jews. He advocated Jewish settlement in Palestine, a phenomenon that in his judgment would not adversely affect the Arabs. Blyden reproved the sons of Abraham for remaining in the Diaspora and for not migrating to their ancient homeland, which the Ottoman Turks were misgoverning.[7] His words advising Jews to repatriate themselves, penned in 1873, would warm the hearts of today's frustrated Jewish Agency officials as they labor, frequently in vain, to promote emigration to Israel.

By the final decades of the nineteenth century, the recrudescence of anti–Semitism both in Russia following the assassination of Czar Alexander II in 1881 and in Western Europe, most notably in France and Germany, had led to a rebirth of political Zionism. Zionist associations planted colonies in Palestine, and Theodor Herzl, a Vienna–based journalist, emerged as the prime mover and central personality of the rejuvenated movement. In 1896 Herzl published his landmark volume, *The Jewish State*, which underlined the hopelessness of assimilation as a solution to the ubiquitous Jewish problem and offered nationhood as a viable alternative. Instead of being a vulnerable minority devoid of power and subject to the ravages of anti–Semitism, Jews would have a country of their own where they would constitute a power–wielding majority of the population.

The following year, 196 delegates from a score of nations representing world Jewry gathered in Basel, Switzerland, to analyze the plight of the Jews and to forge a plan to guide Jewish destiny. One can argue that the first world Zionist Congress established the *national* character of the Jews. Without any doubt, it created a permanent international Zionist organization, the instrument that was to breathe life into a Jewish nation in Palestine in just half a century.

Blyden's response to Herzl's Zionism was set forth in *The Jewish Question*, published the year after the Basel conclave. That twenty-four page booklet, avidly philo–Semitic and philo–Zionist, was dedicated to Louis Solomon, a Jewish acquaintance of Blyden's from his residence in West Africa. Blyden was familiar with Herzl's *Jewish State* and predicted that it propounded ideas that had "given such an impetus to the real work of the Jews as will tell with enormous effect upon their future history."[8] Blyden also commented on the powerful influence of that "tidal wave from Vienna—that inspiration almost Mosaic in its originality and in its tendency, which drew crowds of Israelites to Basel in August 1897...and again in 1898."[9]

Blyden, the Pan–Africanist, recognized Herzl's efforts for the Jews as analogous to his own activities to effect a selective return of Afro–Americans to their homeland. No wonder he described Zionism as "that marvellous movement"[10] and indicated his backing for a Jewish nation. If conditions were propitious in Palestine, the Jewish nation could be located there. Blyden was of the opinion that "there is hardly a man in the civilized world—Christian, Mohammedan, or Jew who does not recognize the claim and right of the Jew to the Holy Land." His enthusiasm for Zionism was unbridled, and he declared there were few "who, if the conditions were favorable would not be glad to see them return in a body and take their place in the land of their fathers as a great—a leading secular power."[11] Zionist pioneers were no less mistaken in expecting a warm welcome from the Arab inhabitants in Zion, but, it must be recalled, that Arab nationalism was in its infancy at the turn of the century.

If conditions were not favorable in Palestine, the Jewish nation could be built elsewhere. By not limiting Zionism's field of operations exclusively to Palestine, Blyden echoed the sentiments of the territorialists such as the Russian–born Leo Pinsker. Pinsker, in 1882, had written a pamphlet called *Auto–Emancipation* in which he argued that "the goal of our present endeavors must not be the 'Holy Land' but a land of our own. We need nothing but a large piece of land for our poor brothers; a piece of land which shall remain our property from which no foreign master can expel us."[12]

Geography was not crucial in Blyden's thoughts about Zionism. He was convinced that the Jewish destiny was not just to establish "a political power in one corner of the earth," but to achieve something far nobler. To the Jews had been "entrusted the spiritual hegemony of mankind."[13] He felt that Jews, along with people of African descent, were specially qualified, by virtue of their heritage of suffering and sorrow, to be spiritual leaders of a materialistic world. With this in mind, he invited Jews to Africa. "...Africa appeals to the Jew...to come with his scientific and other culture, gathered by his exile in many lands, and with his special spiritual endowments," Blyden wrote in 1898.[14]

In a fascinating episode, this quixotic notion was almost fulfilled in 1903 when the British government offered the Zionist Congress territory in Kenya for developing a Jewish colony. The offer came at a time of deteriorating conditions in Russia where the largest masses of downtrodden Jews dwelled. Acquisition of a haven was imperative. With Palestine unavailable, some other place might have to do, at least temporarily. In addition to this humanitarian consideration, Herzl also understood the diplomatic advantage of not rejecting the British offer out of hand. With an international power like Britain treating the Zionist movement as the speaker for world Jewry, Herzl's concept of Jewish nationhood stood closer than ever to realization. A Britain committed to aiding the Zionists would have to provide a substitute for East Africa if the proffered territory proved unsuitable. A Zionist–sponsored commission dispatched to Kenya found it seriously deficient. Palestine–centered Jews had from the start regarded even temporary conditional acceptance of East Africa as tantamount to treason, and the acrimonious dispute over East Africa that ensued made necessary a tormenting reappraisal of the Zionist movement. By 1905 the offer was finally declined. The Zionists were resolutely determined to found a Jewish state in Palestine and only in Palestine.[15]

Most of Blyden's prominent black contemporaries did not share his Pan–Negro fervor or his African orientation. Booker T. Washington emphatically rejected the back–to–Africa movement in favor of a stay–at–home philosophy. For at least twenty years, from 1895 when he delivered his famous Atlanta Exposition address until his death, Booker Taliaferro Washington was the best known black in white America. So great was his celebrity that, although he was born a slave in western Virginia in 1856, he was asked to dine with Theodore Roosevelt in the White House (only once, however, because of howls of racist protest) and invited to take tea with the venerable Queen Victoria. His path to fame was a tortuous one. As a youngster, he suffered numerous privations and often lacked the most basic necessities of life. He had to toil in salt works but was determined to teach himself the alphabet and later managed, despite much hardship, to obtain an education at Hampton Institute. In 1881, with financial help from the Alabama legislature, he founded Tuskegee Institute, which he headed for three and a half decades.

At a time of deteriorating conditions for blacks, when racism was reaching its zenith, Washington, at least in public, exemplified the philosophy of accommodation, of avoiding direct confrontation with the white power structure. In his 1895 Atlanta speech, he appeared to accept the inevitability of racial segregation and described his aggrieved brethren as "the most patient, faithful, law abiding and unresentful people the world has ever seen."[16] Rightly or wrongly, later generations of black Americans came to view Washington's posture as a cringing and groveling one, hardly appropriate at a time when blacks were being disfranchised, Jim Crowed, and lynched.

Washington, like countless other blacks weaned on Scripture, had a "special and peculiar interest in the history and progress of the Jewish race."[17] He frequently drew parallels between the tragic histories of Jews and blacks. Speaking in 1905 to a biracial audience in Little Rock, Arkansas, he opined that ignorance and racial hatred had never solved a single problem and cautioned his black listeners not to become discouraged or despondent because conditions for blacks were becoming worse. "In Russia there are one–half as many Jews as there are Negroes in this country and yet I feel sure that within a month more Jews have been persecuted and killed than the whole number of our people who have been lynched during the past forty years." However, this was no excuse for lynchings, he added.[18] Even if Washington's statistics on the victims of pogroms in czarist Russia were accurate, the comparison must have provided cold comfort to Afro–Americans. In the land of the free and the home of the brave, 60 blacks were lynched in 1905 alone, and from 1889 through 1905, lynch mobs claimed no fewer than 1,707 black victims.[19]

Washington believed that salvation for black Americans would be achieved through thrift and hard work. Racial solidarity would also contribute to black progress. Jews, Washington argued, could serve as a model in this respect. "There is, perhaps, no race that has suffered so much, not so much in America as in some of the countries in Europe. But these people have clung together. They have had a certain amount of unity, pride and love of race," he commented in 1899. He then prophesied—correctly, as future events were to demonstrate—that Jews would become more and more influential in the United States, "a country where they were once despised and looked upon with scorn and derision." Washington admonished blacks to follow the Jewish people in developing faith in themselves. Unless blacks learned to imitate Jews in this respect, he wrote, they could not expect to achieve a high degree of success.[20]

More than a decade later, Washington, who had observed the Jewish condition in diverse locales—in London's East End, in Denmark, Germany, and Austria, in the Russian Pale of Settlement, and in the ghettos of Poland—reiterated this theme. A 1901 manuscript for an article includes his observation that prejudice and persecution notwithstanding, the Jew was advancing largely by dint of education. Jews had struggled to the point where they occupied positions of power and enjoyed pre-eminence in civilization. Washington concluded that the "Negro has much to learn from the Jew."[21]

Undoubtedly, Washington knew about modern political Zionism, but apparently did not take it very seriously. Perhaps he hoped that the Jewish community, the ethnic model to be emulated, would not take it very seriously. When asked in 1910 if there was any back-to-Africa movement among Afro–Americans comparable to the Zionist movement, Washington chuckled and replied, "I think it is with the African pretty much as it is with the Jews, there is a good deal of talk about it, but nothing is done, there is certainly no sign of any exodus to Liberia."[22] Washington was acutely aware of the repatriationist enterprises of Bishop Henry McNeal Turner, the leading apostle of back–to–Africanism in the 1890s and early 1900s,[23] but he could "see no way out of the Negro's present condition in the South by returning to Africa."[24] Washington, who never once visited his African homeland although he found ample time for several trips to Europe, preferred a future for blacks in the United States where a satisfactory racial adjustment would have to be made. Given his staunch opposition to emigration as a solution to the Negro problem, his disinterest in Zionism was predictable.

As far as Zionism was concerned, Washington's flippant remark about Jews paying only lip service to it was half true. Virtually no *American* Jews were sailing to Palestine. In 1910 most Jewish inhabitants of the United States had just arrived from Eastern Europe during the previous two or three decades. On the other hand, the same despair born of resurgent anti–Semitism and chronic poverty that prompted in excess of a million and a half Jews to forsake the czar's realms for Western Europe and the New World furnished the impetus for the Second Aliya. *Aliya,* literally *ascension,* refers to waves of immigration to Palestine. The Second Aliya, stimulated in part by the unsuccessful Russian revolution in 1905 and the concurrent pogroms, was well underway when Washington casually dismissed Zionism as a remedy for Jewish ills. Although numerically small, it brought to Palestine many of those socialist Zionist idealists who would begin to transform the Zionist vision into reality. Those adventurous *chalutzim* (pioneers) were destined to become Israel's establishment, the power elite in the future Jewish state. The fruits of their labor Zionist ideology (for example, the kibbutzim, the moshavim, and the Histadrut or labor federation) are still vital elements in Israel today.

Booker T. Washington died in 1915 during the carnage of World War I. In the midst of that global cataclysm, political Zionism won an important diplomatic victory. Britain was eager to mobilize Jewish opinion in support of the Allied cause. With the new Bolshevik regime extricating itself from the sanguinary morass of the war, Jewish influence in the Soviet Union could be beneficial, or so Britain's Prime Minister David Lloyd George thought. American Zionist sentiment, if properly cultivated, could also prove useful in stimulating the war effort. Therefore, in November of 1917, the British Foreign Minister, Arthur James Balfour, who not coincidentally also had a lifelong interest in Jews and a profound admiration for their culture, issued his famous declaration. Writing to Lord Rothschild, a member of the fabulously wealthy and prestigious international banking family and a leader among British Jewry, Balfour asserted,

> His Majesty's Government view with favour the establishment in Palestine of a national home for the Jewish people, and will use their best endeavours to facilitate the achievement of his object, it being clearly understood that nothing shall be done which may prejudice the civil and religious rights of existing non–Jewish communities in Palestine, or the rights and political status enjoyed by Jews in any other country.[25]

Few people at the time realized that Balfour's promise of a national home for the Jews conflicted both with the 1915 McMahon–Hussein agreement, which the British arranged to incite Arab opposition to the Ottoman Empire, and with the Sykes–Picot agreement allocating Ottoman territory to France, Russia, and Britain. For the Zionist, the Balfour Declaration, which was subsequently incorporated in the League of Nations mandate for Palestine, was a solemn pledge to the Jewish people. For the Arabs, it was treacherous, duplicitous, and illegal.

If anything, racial strife in the United States intensified during and right after the Great War. Lynchings continued unabated in the United States while black troops fought in Europe to make the world safe for democracy. Race riots, which were actually pogroms against black communities, occurred with unprecedented fury and frequency.

In those racially troubled times, the black titan, W.E.B. Du Bois emerged as a champion of Zionism as well as a tireless fighter for racial justice in this country. Even before the advent of World War I, Du Bois was a towering figure whose intellect and dedication to the cause of racial equality inspired hope in oppressed black America and fear and awe among whites.

Born in Great Barrington, Massachusetts, in 1868, Du Bois forged a legendary career both as a scholar and as an activist that spanned almost a century of turbulent racial history. Educated at Fisk University and the University of Berlin, Du Bois later earned a Ph.D. from Harvard. Until his death in Ghana in 1963, his scholarly output was enormous, including historical treatises, incisive sociological studies, and essays on all the important issues of his day.

Du Bois's unflagging efforts as a crusader for first-class citizenship for the black American at least equalled and probably surpassed the importance of his academic accomplishments. Pursuing that lofty and elusive goal, he relentlessly assailed the ears of his fellow citizens for decade after decade. He worked to end lynchings and the humiliation of Jim Crowism. Even before the dawn of the twentieth century, his militant egalitarian philosophy was offered to black Americans as a viable alternative to the racial accommodationism of Booker T. Washington, which Du Bois found demeaning and subversive to black manhood. Du Bois deserves much of the credit for founding the National Association for the Advancement of Colored People (NAACP) in 1910, and he was a driving force behind the Pan–African movement, which concerned itself with the plight of subjugated people of African descent on the African continent and in the far–flung African dispersion.

With the public disclosure of the Balfour Declaration, Du Bois recognized in the exertions of the Zionists a program and policy that could possibly hasten the liberation of Africa. Africa's future, specifically the destiny of territory formerly controlled by Germany, was to be determined after the armistice of November 1918. Du Bois dreamt of an independent free central African state, which minimally would be carved out of German East Africa and the Belgian Congo.[26] If the triumphant Entente powers took into account the wishes of blacks in Africa and elsewhere, the victors would be given an "effective weapon" militating against restoration of African colonies to the vanquished Germans.[27] Alas, Du Bois and his Pan–African cohorts lacked the diplomatic leverage to persuade the Versailles peacemakers to sanction a black African counterpart to the Balfour Declaration.[28]

Du Bois's ideas about the parallel between modern political Zionism and Pan-Africanism were tersely summarized in *Crisis*, the organ of the NAACP, which he edited. Appearing as an editorial in February of 1919 when Du Bois was in France to organize a crucial Pan-African conference, it stated:

The African movement means to us what the Zionist movement must mean to the Jews, the centralization of race effort and the recognition of a racial fount. To help bear the burden of Africa does not mean any lessening of effort in our own problems at home. Rather it means increased interest. For any ebullition of action and feeling that results in an amelioration of the lot of Africa tends to ameliorate the conditions of colored peoples throughout the world. And no man liveth unto himself.[29]

Of course, Du Bois's philo-Zionism should not be seen simply as a political strategy. Nor was it an isolated, haphazard, fleeting thought. Rather, it was in keeping with this general sympathy for the liberation struggles of persecuted peoples around the globe.

As a student in Europe in the the 1890s, Du Bois encountered the virulent bacillus of anti-Semitism in Germany and Poland and came to develop a genuine appreciation of Zionism as a solution to the Jewish problem. That appreciation ripened with the passing years and fully flowered following the Holocaust. In the intervening decades Du Bois closely monitored developments in Palestine under the British mandate.

Even in the pages of *The Brownie's Book*, a monthly magazine for Afro-American children Du Bois started in 1919–1920, several selections dealt with the progress of Zionism. In its very first issue, Du Bois directed the attention of young black readers to the new Jewish state planned in the ancient Holy Land, "'round about Jerusalem."[30] Eight months later he informed his juvenile readership that a "great Zionist congress of the Jews is meeting in London." Du Bois was particularly struck by proposals to "tax the Jews all over the world for the support of the new Jewish government in Palestine."[31] In January of 1921, he observed that blueprints for a Hebrew university on the biblical Mount of Olives in Jerusalem had been completed and remarked on urban planning in the "New Palestine."[32]

For Du Bois, imperial Britain, which had plundered Africa after the unjustified partition of the "dark continent," was the bete noire— or bete blanche, to be precise. England retained many colonies by fostering religious and national jealousies and then presiding as a benevolent arbitrator, Du Bois wrote in his "As the Crow Flies" column published in *Crisis*. He speculated about the reason for what he described as the "murder of Jews by Arabs in Palestine" in 1929.[33] Tensions between Arab and Jew had smoldered for some time because of disagreement over access to the Western Wall in Jerusalem. In August defenseless Jews were massacred in Hebron and Safed by "ruthless and bloodthirsty evil-doers," as the malefactors were characterized by the British high commissioner.[34] That violence merely foreshadowed the bloodletting to come.

Zionism's trials and tribulations also caught the eye of another important black leader, a bitter rival of Du Bois, the redoubtable Marcus Garvey. In 1916, the year before the Balfour Declaration was issued, Garvey arrived in the United States. Though inspired by Booker T. Washington's autobiography, *Up From Slavery*, the Jamaican-born Garvey's solution to the manifold problems that beset black folk differed widely from that of the sage of Tuskegee. Garvey arrived armed with a Pan-Negro, black nationalist ideology that was to captivate millions of blacks on the mother continent as well as in the African Diaspora. In the course of a few years, he built what black historian John Hope Franklin has characterized as the "first and only really mass movement among Negroes in the United States."[35]

The era was a propitious one for his black nationalist crusade. It coincided with an influx of West Indians who constituted the nucleus of Garvey's Universal Negro Improvement Association (UNIA). Moreover, Afro-Americans who had migrated by the hundreds of thousands from the rural South to the urban North expecting a dramatic improvement in their fortunes, if not a racial utopia, were sadly disillusioned. Discrimination in employment and housing knew no regional boundaries, they quickly discovered, and racial violence was commonplace in the frigid North.

Garvey's philosophy of race pride could raise their hopes, lift their spirits, and reinvigorate their sagging self-esteem. Long before the slogan "black is beautiful" became *de rigeur*, Garvey preached the concept that Americans of African descent need not feel ashamed, not of their pigmentation, not of their heritage.

Day in and day out, Garvey advocated the cause of self-determination for Africans, both those at home in Africa and those abroad. Africa was then controlled almost entirely by European colonialists. But Garvey argued that it had to be transformed into a "Negro Empire where every Black man, whether he was born in Africa or in the Western world, will have the opportunity to develop on his own lines under the protection of the most favorable democratic institutions."[36]

Blacks living as minorities in the New World faced bleak futures in Garvey's view, which was strikingly similar to those of the political Zionists regarding Jews in the *galut* (dispersion). Outside the confines of the land of their forebears, "ruin and disaster" awaited Africans. Therefore, Garvey urged that Africa's dispersed and mistreated sons and daughters be restored to her. The stocky, ebony–skinned Jamaican asserted that Africa was the "legitimate, moral and righteous home of all Negroes."[37] But he did not favor an immediate, wholesale repatriation. Even if the wherewithal were available, it would take a half century to largely depopulate the United States. Every black was not wanted anyway. Lazy ones and those lacking self–reliance, for example, were not desired. Those whom Garvey wished to see emigrate to Africa were the adventurous and industrious blacks, such as the members of his UNIA, whose goal was an independent nationality. They numbered six million, Garvey claimed.

Even the stay–at–homes, those blacks who remained outside of Africa, would benefit from the redemption of Africa. Garvey's widow, Amy Jacques Garvey, has explained, "Garvey saw Africa as a *nation* to which the African peoples of the world could look for help and support, moral and physical, when ill–treated or abused for being black."[38] Garveyite rhetoric here virtually duplicates that of the Zionists who argue to this day that a strong Jewish state enhances the security of Jews still in exile.

As a supporter of the back–to–Africa movement, Garvey failed. In 1924 he was conspicuously unsuccessful in his bid to establish settlements in Liberia. The next year the would–be black Moses began to serve a prison term meted out to him following his conviction for using the United States mails to defraud investors in one of his black nationlist commercial enterprises, the Black Star Steamship Line. His remaining days in this country were to be spent in a federal penitentiary in Georgia. After his sentence was commuted in 1927, he was deported to his native Jamaica as an undesirable alien, never to set foot in the United States again.

Throughout his checkered career, Garvey was fond of pointing out the analogies between his brand of black nationalism and other nationalisms, specifically those of the Irish, the East Indians, the Egyptians, and the Jews. For example, in July 1920, Garvey told a UNIA meeting that blacks in the aftermath of World War I were a new people: "A new spirit, a new courage, has come to us simultaneously as it came to other people of the world. It came to us at the same time it came to the Jew. When the Jew said 'We shall have Palestine!' the same sentiment came to us when we said 'We shall have Africa!'"[39]

William H. Ferris, a leading Garveyite who was both an educator and a journalist, repeated this analogy before the same gathering:

> Our position in civilization for the last three hundred years had been the same position which the Jews have occupied during the past 2500 years. The Jews have been scattered all over the world and been suppressed by one race and then another. But the Jews have now realized that it is necessary for them to build up an empire and a republic in their

native land of Palestine. In this stage of the world's history it is necessary for the Negro to build up some sort of republic and empire in Liberia so that there will be some land which he can call his own.[40]

Although Garvey and many of his disciples felt an affinity for Zionism, he sometimes displayed his pique over the shabby treatment accorded black nationalism compared with other nationalist movements. Speaking in London in 1928, he lamented the fact that when the Versailles peacemakers distributed the spoils of the war, "you gave to the Jews, Palestine; you gave to the Egyptians, a large modicum of self-goverment; you gave to the Irish Home Rule Government and Dominion status; you gave the Poles a new Government of their own." When he asked rhetorically what had been given to the Negro, an anonymous voice rang out from the throng gathered at London's Royal Albert Hall. "Nothing," it said.[41] It is clear, though, that Garvey's animosity was not directed at the Zionists or the Egyptian nationalists, the Polish patriots or the Irish home rulers, but at Britain and the other European powers that denied Africans the right to their continent.

Garveyite philo-Zionism was sometimes reciprocated. Louis Michael, a Jew from Los Angeles, sent the UNIA a telegram in August 1920 that read, "As a Jew, a Zionist and a Socialist I join heartily and unflinchingly in your historical movement for the reclamation of Africa. There is no justice and no peace in the world until the Jew and the Negro both control side by side Palestine and Africa."[42]

Garvey stirred the curiosity of much of the Yiddish press in the United States. His followers and ideas received accolades from pro-Zionist Yiddish newspapers such as the *Morgen Journal* and the *Tageblatt*, which saw the UNIA as a kindred nationalist undertaking. These publications sometimes applied Zionist nomenclature to Garvey's movement. To cite one illustration, Garvey's anthem, "Ethiopia—Thou Land of Our Fathers," composed by Arnold Ford, a West Indian-born black rabbi and Garvey apostle, was dubbed "The Negro Hatikvah." "Hatikvah," or "Hope," was the Zionist anthem and is now the national anthem of Israel.[43]

Despite his support for Zionism, an example he urged his followers to emulate, Garvey harbored ambivalent feelings about Jews. He believed the Jews' obsession with money was the root of their difficulties in Germany and later in Palestine.[44] He subscribed to more than one unflattering stereotype of Jews and had been guilty of anti-Semitic utterances at his trial, over which a Jewish jurist, Judge Julian Mack, had presided. But to label him as an anti-Semite is to be guilty of gross oversimplification.

Initially at least, Garvey seems not to have recognized the dangers posed by Adolph Hitler's accession to power. It is indeed unfortunate that in this respect the Jamaican was not unique. Garvey admired the Fuhrer as a German patriot, a fervent nationalist but one who had outrageously mistreated the Jews and was antagonistic towards blacks.[45] In 1935 Garvey prophesied that it was only a matter of time before the Jews destroyed Nazi Germany as they had allegedly destroyed Russia. "Jewish finance is a powerful world factor," Garvey observed. "It can destroy men, organizations and nations," he added with considerable hyperbole.[46] Yet in the pages of *The Blackman*, his monthly journal published for a short while in Jamaica and then beginning in the spring of 1935 in London, Garvey frequently expressed his sympathy for Jews as a despised and oppressed minority.[47] He lauded their efforts to rebuild their Zion in Palestine as he had done years before in his American heyday. Praise was due the Jews because they recognized the "only safe thing to do is to go after and establish racial autonomy." So wrote the Black Moses in 1936.[48]

By 1936 Palestine was in turmoil. Rioting and sporadic fighting claimed both Arab and Jewish lives. Persecution by Hitler had escalated *aliya* from Germany and Austria, to which certain Palestinian Arab leaders voiced strenuous objections. A general strike was called, aiming at terminating the immigration of Jews and halting their further purchase of land. It too was marked by bloodshed.

Faced with a rapidly worsening state of affairs, the British appointed a commission of inquiry, one of several that sought, to no avail, to reconcile conflicting Jewish and Arab aspirations in the Holy Land. In their report, made public in July of 1937, the so-called Peel Commission advocated that the country be partitioned into a British mandatory zone, an Arab state, and a Jewish state. Arab opinion overwhelmingly opposed partition, but the Zionists were divided, some believing that half a loaf was better than none.

Writing from Britain in the twilight of his career, Garvey admonished the Jews not to throw away their opportunity to establish a state of their own. What was important was not the size of a Jewish state but the chance to have an independent government that could enjoy diplomatic and economic relations with other nations. Garvey speculated that the black man's case for a country might be strengthened by the success of the Jewish cause. In Garvey's judgment, the Negro had even "more right to a free state of his own in Africa than the Jew in Palestine." Unwillingness by blacks to line up behind the UNIA the way Jews supported Zionism explained why the world did not take the black seriously.[49]

Territorial compromise, as recommended by the Peel Commission, did not bring peace to Palestine. Arab–Jewish frictions did not diminish in the late 1930s as ominous war clouds gathered over Europe and the plight of German Jewry was further aggravated. In May of 1939 publication of the British "White Paper" dealt a cruel blow to Zionist hopes. At the very moment when the need for refuge was most desperate, the British, in response to Arab agitation, decided to curtail Jewish immigration to Palestine. Only seventy–five thousand Jews would be admitted over the five–year period. Jewish land purchases were restricted as well. British policy in Palestine on the eve of World War II, clearly calculated to mollify the Arabs, had the tragic effect of denying sanctuary to untold numbers of Jewish refugees in flight from Nazism.

Whereas an influx of Jews into Palestine would have heightened tensions in the troubled land and added to the herculean task of Britain's maintaining the peace, diverting a productive white population to British Guiana would have strengthened the British position there. Consequently, Prime Minister Neville Chamberlain announced in May of 1939 that his government would contemplate the settlement of Jewish refugees in that South American colony. Garvey reacted with alacrity and anger. In this instance, black rights were being subordinated to those of Jews. British Guiana was a "Negro country," Garvey exclaimed, a description with which the sizeable East Indian community would have vehemently disagreed. Jews had no claim on Guiana and their presence there would only serve to turn blacks and Jews into enemies. The correct goal for Jews was a Jewish nation, but not in Guiana, which Garvey insisted was the property of blacks. Garvey was so incensed by the Guiana plan and so irritated by what he perceived as British concern with Jews, he commented that an injustice had been done the Arab in Palestine. Ostensibly, Garvey's endorsement of Zionism was predicated on the notion that Zionism's chief value was as a model for victimized Diaspora blacks to copy.[50] When it appeared to pre–empt black rights, it earned his animosity. In June 1940, Garvey died in London in relative obscurity. As for Guiana, it never materialized as a refuge for Jews. Indeed, precious few havens were available at that critical juncture in the history of the Jews. After Hitler's invasion of Poland on September 1, 1939, it grew increasingly difficult for Jews to escape. The lives of millions, especially those dwelling in eastern Europe, were imperiled by the Fuhrer's mad racial themes.

Early in 1941, W.E.B. Du Bois wrote that American Jews were proposing to raise millions of dollars for Palestine, "the only refuge that the harassed Jewry of Europe had today." Although Jews didn't really believe in segregation, they were going to make segregation in Palestine both possible and profitable and simultaneously work for an unsegregated humanity. In the process, Zionism provided blacks who believed "someone else is going to do our fighting for us" with a constructive lesson in self–help. It is regettable that during the war the Zionists were incapable of opening the gates of Palestine to those few harassed European Jews who managed to slip through the Nazi grip.[51]

When the war ended in 1945, a stunned world learned the grisly truth about the Holocaust, which dramatized, as no event in modern history has, the necessity for a Jewish homeland. Hitler had unwittingly convinced skeptics of the logic of Zionism. The converts included most Diaspora Jews who, until then, had been lukewarm at best and downright hostile at worst towards the Zionist movement.

World War II also dealt a serious blow to the British empire after 1945. Britain was more favorably disposed to relinquish parts of the empire, particularly when they were costly and troublesome owing to local agitation for independence. Palestine was a case in point. Arab–Jewish strife had not vanished miraculously. In fact, as the Jewish claim for unlimited immigration to Palestine by Holocaust survivors grew more raucous, Arabs felt still more threatened.

By 1947, Britain, caught between the conflicting claims of Arab and Jew, was not just willing to depart from Palestine. It was eager to leave and consequently presented its dilemma to the young United Nations. The plan eventually adopted by the United Nations called for the partition of Palestine into an independent sovereign Jewish state and an independent sovereign Arab state. There was to be a third entity: an international zone under United Nations trust, which would encompass Jerusalem and its suburbs, including Bethlehem. Despite vociferous Arab objections to a plan they deemed unfair and unworkable, the General Assembly voted for it as a means of reconciling the seemingly irreconcilable national aspirations of the two peoples. Support from two–thirds of the members voting was necessary for approval. Only frantic eleventh–hour lobbying by Zionist sympathizers made possible the resulting vote: thirty–three for, thirteen against, ten abstaining.[52]

One Afro–American who was lobbied intensively and heavy-handedly by advocates of partition was Walter White, the fair-skinned executive director of the NAACP. Zionists hoped White could persuade two black nations, Haiti and Liberia, to reverse their previously announced anti–partition stance. In his autobiography, White recounted his doubts about both the "wisdom and practicability" of dividing the territory in dispute. But no other feasible solution had been advanced. As an unflagging believer in racial integration, White "did not like the self–segregation of Zionism, nor...approve of the attitude of many Jews who had made it a sacred cult." White took umbrage at some of the Zionist pressure, which he found imperious and racially condescending. Nevertheless, his reluctance notwithstanding, he supported partition "because Palestine seemed the only haven anywhere in the world for nearly one million Jews of Europe."[53] In the end, Liberia, Haiti, and the Philippines, whom White had also attempted to influence, voted for the United Nations resolution. As matters turned out, their votes were crucial to the creation of Israel. After a gestation period of approximately half a century, the Jewish homeland of which Herzl had written and dreamt would become a reality. The Rubicon had been crossed, if not the Jordan.

In the months following the fateful November 1947 United Nations vote to partition Palestine, there was a resurgence of battling between Jews and Palestinian Arabs. Jews in the *Yishuv* were jubilant to learn that after two thousand years, a Jewish state would re-emerge in at least a portion of their ancient homeland. By contrast, Arabs were livid. They constituted a sizeable majority—two-thirds in fact, of Palestine's entire population, and they believed Zionist intrigue had caused the world body to forsake them. Arabs vented their spleen by attacking Jews, who then retaliated in kind. Civil war threatened to violently tear the country asunder, the very state of affairs the United Nations had sought to avoid.

Although outnumbered, the Jews were better organized and their community services operated more efficiently than those of the Arabs, many of whose leaders fled to safer Arab locales. The Jewish armies proved superior as well. Atrocities committed by both sides punctuated the bitter fighting. Word spread quickly of the notorious Deir Yacin Massacre of Arabs near Jerusalem in April 1948 and led to panic among the already anxious and often leaderless Arabs. This panic touched off the exodus of terrified Palestinians and, in large measure, created the still unresolved Arab refugee problem. When the war finally ended at the beginning of 1949, approximately three quarters of a million Palestinians found themselves in the Arab countries surrounding the triumphant "Zionist entity."

When the British withdrew and at long last extricated themselves from the Palestine morass, military forces of five Arab nations—Iraq, Jordan, Lebanon, Egypt, and Syria—invaded the fledgling Jewish state David Ben–Gurion had proclaimed on May 14, 1948. What had earlier been a civil war broadened into an international conflict. Given their vast manpower, the Arabs prophesied a quick victory, but as a result of poor coordination among the Arab commanders and low morale among their troops, the anticipated triumph eluded them.

In the midst of the sanguinary first Arab–Israeli war, Israel's fate became entwined with the career of an extraordinary black American—Ralph Johnson Bunche. When Count Folke Bernadotte, the Swedish diplomat serving as the United Nations mediator, was assassinated by members of the extremist Stern Gang in September of 1948, Bunche, who had been secretary of the peacekeeping Palestine Commission, was appointed acting mediator.

Born in Detroit in 1904, Bunche as a youth was outstanding both as a scholar and an athlete. He was the first black American to earn a doctorate in political science, which he received from Harvard in 1934. He subsequently assisted Swedish scholar Gunnar Myrdal in researching his monumental opus on the Afro–American, *An Ameri-*

can Dilemma.[54] In the early 1940s, Bunche had argued that anti-Semitism among blacks and the irrational fear and dislike of blacks on the part of Jews were nonsensical examples of the pot calling the kettle black. He expressed a hope that Jewish and black leaders and organizations would strive to improve the strained relations that existed between the two minorities. "In large measure," he maintained, "their problems—their grievances and their fears are cut to a common pattern."[55]

Bunche's statesmanship facilitated the termination of the first Arab–Israeli war. Ensconced in his headquarters on the Greek island of Rhodes, Bunche mediated negotiations between King Farouk's Egypt and Israel, resulting in an armistice agreement in February 1949.[56] Agreements between Israel and other Arab belligerents were also concluded. For his efforts in hastening the end of hostilities, Bunche became in 1950 the first Afro–American awarded the Nobel Peace Prize.

On at least one occasion, the fact that Bunche was a black American colored his outlook on the clash between Arabs and Jews. When matters were still precarious in Palestine, Bunche thought it advisable to consult Menachem Begin, who was then the wanted chieftain of the Irgun, an underground "terrorist" faction. After a clandestine meeting between United Nations officials and those of the Irgun, Begin thanked Bunche for his diligence and toil in preparing a report on their dialogue.[57] In his personal memoir, *The Revolt*, the future prime minister characterized Bunche as the warmest of the United Nations team. As Begin remembered the conclusion of their meeting, Bunche shook his hand and exclaimed emotionally, "I can understand you. I am also a member of a persecuted minority."[58] Begin also paid tribute to Bunche as "undoubtedly a brilliant mind."[59]

Bunche's mediating role nurturing Israel in its fragile infancy is also recalled by Afro–Americans who not infrequently invoke his name to justify black involvement in the Middle East conflict.[60] However, in 1978, one black columnist bewailed the fact that "although there are monuments in New York to Bunche, not one stands to his memory in Israel. Not even a tree."[61]

In view of Bunche's contribution, it is hard to believe that as late as the fall of 1948, his work as mediator in Palestine was judged insufficiently pro–Zionist by the erudite W.E.B. Du Bois. Speaking to the American Jewish Congress on November 30 of that year, Du Bois apologized in the name of fifteen million black Americans for "the apparent apostasy of Ralph Bunche...to the clear ideas of freedom and fair play, which should have guided the descendant of an American slave." Count Bernadotte, who represented the nefarious combination of European aristocracy and American money to Du Bois, could not be expected to "judge Israel justly and without bias." But from Bunche, Du Bois hoped for more than consistent adherence to State Department directives that prevented him from playing "a great role for freedom." In Du Bois's estimation, the State Department was guilty of compromise, vacillation, and betrayal. On the other hand, he had hoped that Bunche "would have stood fast for justice, freedom and the good faith of his nation and race."[62]

Even before the Nazis capitulated, Du Bois, as editor of *Phylon*, wrote that millions of Jews had perished in Hitler's pogroms and millions more were in peril of extermination. America's doors had been closed to Jewish immigrants and, worse still, "Great Britain has assumed the right to limit Jewish migration to Palestine and to support the nationalism of the Arabs."[63]

From Du Bois's prolific pen came articles and columns trumpeting the cause of the Zionists in their hour of need. In the wake of the Holocaust, Du Bois wrote that there "was one refuge, a little thing, a little corner of the world where the Jews anciently had lived."[64] A Zionist homeland in Palestine was a *sine qua non* for displaced and homeless Jews. There was no other place for them. Persecution was the only real alternative to migration to Zion. In a 1948 piece published as "A Case for the Jews," Du Bois depicted the objective of the Zionist movement as a question of "young and forward thinking Jews, bringing a new civilization into an old land and building up that land out of the ignorance, disease and poverty into which it had fallen, and by democratic methods to build a new and peculiarly fateful modern state."[65]

Du Bois excoriated the British Foreign Secretary, Ernest Bevin, for his "half hidden dislike of Jews," for reneging on the Balfour Declaration, for using British troops against the Jews, for training Arab soldiers for future use against them, and for using the Royal Navy to block the immigration into Palestine of displaced persons.[66] Uprooted Jews were being allowed to rot in Europe while the United States discussed "unworkable possibilities for the partition of Palestine," wrote Du Bois, employing words that echoed the sentiments of the Vladimir Jabotinsky–Begin Revisionists, who envisioned a Jewish state on both banks of the Jordan River.[67]

Du Bois further castigated President Harry Truman for not keeping his promise to back the establishment of a Jewish state and for not allowing weapons to be dispatched to the beleaguered Jews. Because of "sordid commercial" factors, Britain betrayed the Zionists in tandem with the United States. Under intense pressure from the State Department, which was eager to safeguard Middle East oil supplies and apprehensive about potential Soviet penetration of the Arab world, Truman had vacillated. United States repudiation of its position on partition and substitution of a United Nations trusteeship were seriously contemplated for a while. "If there is one act for which President Truman and his advisors can be utterly and finally condemned and refused the support of all decent thinking people, it is this reversal of stand in the matter of Palestine," Du Bois wrote in an ariticle for the black press.[68] Between April 30, 1948, when Du Bois mailed the article to the *Chicago Defender,* and its publication on May 15, 1948, Truman reversed himself again and came out in favor of the Zionist demands. Indeed, the United States was the first nation to extend official recognition to Israel.

Du Bois was closely associated with Jews in the creation of the NAACP, which in June of 1948 expressed its gratification that Israel had come into being. At its 39th annual conference held in Kansas City, Missouri, on June 26, the NAACP adopted the following resolution: "The valiant struggle of the people of Israel for independence serves as an inspiration to all persecuted people throughout the world. We hail the establishment of the new State of Israel and welcome it into the family of nations."[69]

By no means was Du Bois the only black militant with a reputation for challenging tyranny against great odds who was counted among the sympathizers of Zionism. During his time, there were many in the Afro–American community. Take Paul Robeson, for instance. Truly versatile, Robeson was an all–American football player at Rutgers University, an attorney, an accomplished actor, and a soul–stirring vocalist. Until he openly professed his affinity for the Soviet Union and for Communism, Robeson was a national hero, venerated by millions and held up by the United States government as an example of the heights to which a talented, industrious black could rise. During the Cold War, however, Robeson was *persona non grata* and was denied a passport.

Robeson, whose father was a slave, was by his own admission especially close to the Jewish people.[70] On many occasions he took uncompromising stands against the evil of anti–Semitism and the persecution of the Jews. In 1933 he sang in Britain to aid Jewish refugee children, and after the war he witnessed the horrors of Dachau firsthand.[71] Robeson saw Jews as a "race without a nation," and in March 1948, speaking in Honolulu, he said that should an all–out war start in Palestine, he would travel there to sing for the Jewish troops just as he had entertained the anti–Franco Loyalists during the Spanish Civil War. To Robeson this intention was in keeping with his ongoing worldwide fight for the oppressed.[72]

When the Palestine question came before the United Nations in 1947, it received some space in the black press. But then as now there was no unanimity of opinion among black Americans. For example, columnist George Schuyler called upon blacks to follow the model of Zionism. At the same time, he took Palestinian Jews to task for their "imperialistic spirit" and "Hitler–like" methods. Jews, Schuyler argued, had "no more claim on Palestine than the Alpha Kappa Alpha." It was the "Arab aborigines" tarbrushed with Negro blood who were truly entitled to the land. The Bible, which he called the "Jewish *Mein Kampf*," provided no justification whatsoever for Zionism.[73] Procuring the Holy Land was only the immediate objective of the Zionists, he informed his readers. Their long–range goal was to once again build a great political state and "to become one of the richest and most powerful groups in the world today."[74] Such strong sentiments were rarely expressed by the black press and, as far as can be determined, virtually never by black leaders.

Schuyler, who was something of an iconoclast and later became a leading—perhaps the pre-eminent—black conservative in the United States, denied the accusation made by several "Zionist fanatics" that he was anti–Semitic. He added that Arabs are "far more Semitic than most of the Zionists now in Palestine or abroad."[75] Of course, the scholarly Schuyler was playing linguistic tricks. He knew full well that the term *anti–Semitic* referred to animosity towards Jews and the fact that both Hebrew and Arabic are classified as Semitic languages was quite irrelevant.

It is significant that in March of 1948, the *Pittsburgh Courier*, which had carried Schuyler's columns, published a long editoral in which it argued strongly for the legitimacy of a Jewish state. Entitled "Persecution and Doubletalk," the editoral demanded that "the lust for Arabian oil" not be allowed to interfere with the United Nations' pledge to partition Palestine. "Not only do the Jews have the legal right to a part of Palestine based on years of international commitments," the editorial stated, "they also deserve the heartfelt sympathy and support of everyone who hates cruelty and tyranny."[76]

As the foregoing indicates, most black leaders, especially black nationalists, were initially sympathetic to the Zionist movement. Several urged blacks to emulate it. Only the Black Muslims, who identified with their religious counterparts in the Arab world, consistently displayed animosity towards Zionism. They continue to do so right up to the present time. After the Six Day War of June 1967, Israel lost much support among black nationalists and others regarded as "radicals" by white America.

As a result of the Six Day War, a new configuration of power seemed to exist in the Middle East. Because of the enormity and swiftness of the Israeli victory, the image of vulnerability that the Jewish state had projected to much of the outside world since 1948 was now grossly distorted. Although twenty Arab states were still arrayed in opposition to its very existence, Israel was no longer perceived as the engulfed underdog. Its physical annihilation, a real threat prior to June 1967, appeared to be only a very remote possibility thereafter. After 1967, Israel was an expanding nation, an occupying power ruling over hundreds of thousands of Arabs in Gaza and in Judea and

Samaria, the biblical names by which the Israelis called the West Bank. For countless millions of onlookers, David had suddenly become Goliath, the superpower of the region. Who could sympathize with the new Middle Eastern Goliath? Some blacks whose relationship with the gargantuan white Goliath of America had been that of horse to rider found it increasingly difficult to do so. Their hostility toward Israel, America's surrogate in their view, was made explicit. Although Israel has received considerable support from the black caucus in the House of Representatives, in recent years fewer blacks have viewed Zionism as "that marvellous movement."

Notes

1. Hollis R. Lynche, *Edward Wilmot Blyden, Pan–Negro Patriot, 1832–1912* (London: Oxford University Press, 1967), p. vii.

2. Edward W. Blyden, *The Jewish Question* (Liverpool: Lionel Hart, 1898), p. 6. Also see Hollis R. Lynch, "A Black Nineteenth Century Response to Jews and Zionism: The Case of Edward W. Blyden, 1832–1912," unpublished paper presented at the spring symposium of the Afro–American Studies Program of the University of Pennsylvania, March 25–27, 1982.

3. Blyden, *Jewish Question*, p. 6.

4. One proto–Zionist, whose ideas and efforts were generally scorned or ignored, was a Serbian–born rabbi, Yehudah Alkalai. Writing in the 1940s, Alkalai likened Jewish residence outside Palestine to life on the edge of a volcano. He anticipated the World Zionist Congress by almost half a century when he spoke of a representative body for world Jewry. See Yehuda Alkalai, "The Third Redemption," *The Zionist Idea*, ed. Arthur Hertzberg (Garden City, N.Y.: Doubleday, Herzl Press, 1959), pp. 105–107.

5. Zvi Hirsch Kalischer, "Seeking Zion," *The Zionist Idea*, ed. Arthur Hertzberg, pp. 111–114.

6. Moses Hess, *Rome and Jerusalem—A Study in Jewish Nationalism*, trans. Meyer Waxman (New York: Bloch Publishing, 1945).

7. Lynch, "A Black Nineteenth Century Response to Jews and Zionism," p. 7. See Edward W. Blyden, *From West Africa to Palestine* (Freetown, Manchester, and London, 1873), pp. 192–193, 199.

8. Blyden, *Jewish Question*, p. 7.

9. Ibid., p. 8.

10. Ibid., p. 7.

11. Ibid., p. 8.

12. Leo Pinsker, *Auto–Emancipation* (Masada Youth Zionist Organization, 1935), p. 22.

13. Blyden, *Jewish Question*, p. 8.

14. Ibid., p. 23.

15. For the full story of the East African episode in early Zionist history, see Robert G. Weisbord, *African Zion—The Attempt to Es-*

tablish a Jewish Colony in the East Africa Protectorate, 1903–1905 (Philadelphia: Jewish Publication Society, 1968).

16. Booker T. Washington, "The Atlanta Exposition Address," in *Booker T. Washington and His Critics—The Problem of Negro Leadership*, ed. Hugh Hawkins (Boston: D.C. Heath, 1962), p. 16.

17. Louis Harlan, ed., *Booker T. Washington Papers*, vol. 11 (Champagne–Urbana: University of Illinois Press, 1972), p. 390.

18. From an account by Emmett J. Scott in the *Boston Evening Transcript*, December 4, 1905. Ibid., vol. 8, p. 442.

19. *Thirty Years of Lynching in the United States, 1889–1918* (New York: National Association for the Advancement of Colored People, 1919), p. 28.

20. Booker T. Washington, *The Future of the American Negro* (New York: Negro Universities Press, 1969), pp. 181–183.

21. Harlan, ed., *Booker T. Washington Papers*, vol. 11, pp. 390–397.

22. Ibid., vol. 10, p. 382.

23. After Bishop Turner dispatched two boatloads of Afro–Americans to Liberia, Washington said that whites were mistaken in concluding that a majority of blacks were committed to returning to Africa. See Washigton, *The Future of the American Negro*, pp. 163–164.

24. Ibid., p. 159.

25. Don Peretz, *The Middle East Today* (New York: Holt, Rinehart and Winston, 1978), p. 101.

26. *Crisis* 15 (January 1918): 114.

27. *W.E.B. Du Bois Papers* (University of Massachusetts, Amherst, microfilm), reel 6, frame 1,096.

28. See Robert A. Hill, "Jews and the Enigma of the Pan–African Congress of 1919," unpublished paper presented at the spring symposium of the Afro–American Studies Program at the University of Pennsylvania, March 25–27, 1982.

29. *Crisis* 17 (February 1919): 166.

30. Herbert Aptheker, ed., *Writings in Periodicals Edited by W.E.B. Du Bois—Selections from the Brownie's Book* (Millwood, N.J.: Kraus–Thomson, 1980), p. 6, from *The Brownie's Book* 1, no. 1 (January 1920): 23–25.

31. Ibid., p. 52. See *The Brownie's Book* 1, no. 8 (August 1920): 234–235.

32. Ibid., p. 83. See *The Brownie's Book* 2, no. 1 (January 1921): 16–17.

33. *Crisis* 36 (October 1929): 329.

34. Walter Laqueur, *A History of Zionism* (New York: Holt, Rinehart and Winston, 1972), p. 256.

35. John Hope Franklin, *From Slavery to Freedom* (New York: Vintage Books, 1969), p. 492.

36. Amy Jacques Garvey, ed., *Philosophy and Opinions of Marcus Garvey, Or Africa for the Africans* (London: Frank Cass, 1967), p. 53.

37. Ibid., p. 122.

38. Beverly Reed, "Black, Beautiful and Free," *Ebony,* June 1971, p. 48.

39. Robert A. Hill, ed., *Marcus Garvey Papers* (University of California, Los Angeles), originally published in Garvey's organ, *The Negro World,* July 17, 1925.

40. Ibid., see the report of the UNIA meeting in *The Negro World,* July 31, 1920.

41. "The Case of the Negro for International Racial Adjustment, Before the English People" (speech delivered by Marcus Garvey at Royal Albert Hall, London, England, June 6, 1928), pp. 17–18,.

42. Hill, ed., *Marcus Garvey Papers.* This telegram was read at a rally by Garvey. It is contained in a report of a Madison Square Garden Meeting in the *Negro World Convention Bulletin* 3 (August 1920).

43. Hasia R. Diner, *In the Almost Promised Land—American Jews and Blacks, 1915-1935* (Westport, Conn.: Greenwood Press, 1972) pp. 54–55, 76.

44. *The Blackman* 2, no. 2 (July–August 1936): 3.

45. Ibid., 1, no. 1 (December 1933): 2; and 1, no. 4 (March–April 1934): 2–3.

46. Ibid., 1, no. 9 (late July 1935): 9.

47. Ibid., 1, no. 9 (August–September 1935): 10.

48. Ibid., 1, no. 12 (late March 1936): 3.

49. Ibid., 2, no. 7 (August 1937): 2.

50. Ibid., 4, no. 1 (June 1939): 5–6. Less than a year earlier he did not remark on possible injustice perpetrated against Arabs. In a speech delivered in Nova Scotia, he simply stated, "Our obsession is like that of the Jews. They are working for Palestine. We are working for Africa..." (Ibid., 3, no. 10 [July 1938]: 10).

51. *W.E.B. Du Bois Papers,* reel 84, frames 324 and 325. These ideas were published in the New York *Amsterdam News,* January 25, 1941.

52. For the atmosphere of the United Nations at the time, see Peter Grose, "The Partition of Palestine 35 Years Ago," *New York Times Magazine,* November 28, 1982, p. 88ff.

53. Walter White, *A Man Called White—The Autobiography of Walter White* (New York: The Viking Press, 1948), p. 353.

54. Gunnar Myrdal, *An American Dilemma,* 2 vols. (New York: McGraw–Hill, 1964).

55. Lunabelle Wedlock, *The Reaction of Negro Publications and Organizations to German Anti-Semitism* (Washington, D.C.: Howard University Press, 1942), pp. 8, 10.

56. J.C. Hurewitz, *The Struggle for Palestine* (New York: Schocken Books, 1976), p. 319.

57. Menachem Begin, *The Revolt* (New York: Dell, 1978), p. 388.

58. Ibid., pp. 393–394.

59. Ibid., p. 387.

60. See the editorial, "Middle East Powder Keg," in the New York *Amsterdam News*, October 20, 1973.

61. Bill Lane, "people—places 'n' situwayshuns," *Los Angeles Sentinel*, April 6, 1978.

62. Unpublished speech on "America's Responsibility to Israel," delivered November 30, 1948, *W.E.B. Du Bois Papers*, reel 80, frame 1158.

63. "Jews and Arabs," *Phylon* 5, no. 1 (1944): 86. Zionism provided blacks who believed "someone is going to do our fighting for us" with a constructive lesson in self-help, thought Du Bois early in 1941.

64. *W.E.B. Du Bois Papers*, reel 83, frames 1,543 and 1,544. See Du Bois, "Winds of Time," *Chicago Defender*, May 15, 1948.

65. *W.E.B. Du Bois Papers*, reel 82, frame 575. The manuscript, entitled "The Ethics of the Problem of Palestine," was retitled "A Case for the Jews" in the *Chicago Star*, May 8, 1948.

66. Ibid.

67. Ibid., reel 83, frames 1,543 and 1,544.

68. Ibid.

69. *NAACP Papers* (Washington, D.C.: Library of Congress) film 246, reel 12, part 1.

70. See the author's foreword to Paul Robeson, *Here I Stand* (Boston: Beacon Press, 1958), p. 4.

71. Philip Foner, ed., *Paul Robeson Speaks—Writings, Speeches, Interviews, 1918–1974* (New York: Bruner/Mazel Publishers, 1978), p. 462.

72. Ibid., p. 183.

73. *Pittsburgh Courier*, May 24, 1947.

74. Ibid., December 27, 1947.

75. Ibid., March 27, 1948.

76. Ibid., March 13, 1948.

Chapter 8

Judaism and Christianity: Sources of Convergence

Jack D. Spiro

I who speak and you who judge of what I say are mortals, so that on these subjects we should be satisfied with a likely story and demand nothing.

Timaeus

Introduction: Discontinuity

In one of the most thoughtful books on Jewish–Christian relations, A. Roy Eckardt writes, "Jewish faith and Christian faith are radically divergent; Jewish faith and Christian faith are radically the same."[1] While I am not at all certain about the validity of radicalness in either case, I have no doubts that both divergence and similarity do exist. This essay will concentrate primarily on the latter, Jewish–Christian similarities, affinities, mutualities, and continuities. But I would be less than honest if I disregarded the first part of Eckardt's statement. I believe in both, and I must at least mention some ideas that are not only radically but irreconcilably divergent.

Some persuasive writers do not accept the second part of Eckardt's statement. Freedman, for example, takes the position that "to assert Christianity is to deny Judaism," while the assertion of Judaism is the same as the rejection of Christianity.[2] Such a statement, cogently argued, makes the position of commonality seem infeasible.

A similar position is taken by Levi Olan who states unequivocally that "dialogue is both impossible and vain."[3] He presents the arguments of many Christians and Jews who have tried with good intentions to show ways the two traditions might be reconciled. But in virtually every instance, the admission is made that Judaism is still incomplete without Christianity. It is this key factor, according to Olan, that makes reconciliation impossible: "The idea that Judaism is deficient in answering man's personal needs is certainly not acceptable to a Jew.... To a Jew, Judaism contains the answer to man's

---

A version of this chapter originally appeared in *Religious Education* 76, No. 6 (Nov.–Dec. 1981), pp. 605–625. Reprinted by permission of the Religious Education Association.

need. There is no dichotomy between the personal and the social in Judaism.... To a Jew, Judaism is the total answer."[4]

While Christians may believe that Christianity is incomplete without Judaism, primarily because of Hebraic "patrimony," Jews have no reason to feel Judaism is incomplete minus a Christian component. Making a very special attempt to find ways that we are similar seems to imply an element of inseparability between us. While Christians may feel a sense of inseparability, Jews do not. In response to an essay by Paul Tillich, Heller wrote, "When we consider that the Judaic tradition was fed by tributaries which had their source in non-Jewish cultures, may not one speak of an Assyro–Hebraic, a Judeo–Islamic, or a Judeo–Hellenic tradition with equal cogency that one speaks of a Judeo–Christian tradition?"[5]

Olan states that no dialogue is possible as long as Christianity is considered to be the completion of Judaism. But Arthur Cohen goes even further in terms of radical divergence, saying, "We can learn much from the history of Jewish–Christian relations, but the one thing we cannot make of it is a discourse of community, fellowship, and understanding. How then do we make of it a tradition?"[6] Cohen argues that the idea of a Judeo–Christian tradition is a myth. It did not exist as a concept throughout the centuries. In fact, according to Robert Gordis, it was not until the "first half of the 20th century that the concept of 'the Judeo–Christian tradition' or 'the Judeo–Christian heritage' came to flower."[7]

The growing trend throughout this century of speaking about a common tradition "suggests the presence of something else,"[8] especially since the major characteristic of Jewish–Christian relations prior to the twentieth century was that of dispute, apology, and polemic. The traditional Christian position, for many centuries, was expressed in the Catholic doctrine of *nulla salus extra Ecclesiam.*

The something else that Cohen perceives in the present is the threat, common to both Judaism and Christianity, of American secularism. Out of this threat the myth was born: "The Judeo–Christian tradition is an eschatological myth for the Christian who no longer can deal with actual history and a historical myth for Jews who can no longer deal with the radical negations of eschatology." Judaism and Christianity have therefore "made common cause before a world that regards them as hopelessly irrelevant and meaningless. The myth, then, is a projection of the will to endure of both Jews and Christians, an identification of common enemies, an abandonment of millennial antagonisms in the face of threats which do not discriminate between Judaism and Christianity."[9]

Perhaps Cohen's idea of the myth is valid, particularly when we return to the Christian belief in the incompleteness of Judaism. This idea is not an interpretation; it is stated explicitly in the New Testament where we read that "Christ has obtained a ministry which is as much more excellent than the old as the covenant he mediates is better, since it is enacted on a better promise. For if that first covenant had been faultless, there would have been no occasion for a second." Furthermore, Jesus "is the mediator of a new covenant, so that those who are called may receive the promised eternal inheritance, since a death has occurred which redeems them from the transgressions under the first covenant." [10]

A man once came up to me at a meeting on Jewish–Baptist dialogue and introduced himself as a convert from Judaism to Christianity. He called himself a "complete Jew" because he was a Christian. Robert Aron tells a similar tale:

> One day as I was invited to speak about Judaism in a community of monks, the atmosphere was fervent and friendly and the abbot, with the best of intentions, suggested that I visit a young monk in his cell. He was of Jewish descent and recently converted. I was somewhat taken aback, but went to meet the young fellow, sincere and relaxed. He assured me he never felt so Jewish as now since he had become a Christian! [11]

The Church is called "the new people of God." What about the "old," what about the Jews who do not accept Christianity? W.D. Davies answers the question in the following passage:

> ...The Old Testament is the record of God's attempts to prepare for Himself a peculiar people that should make known His ways.
>
> But what is true of Judaism is also true of Christianity. In the New and in the Old Testament God's purposes are to be achieved through a community—the New Israel of God, the church. [12]

To qualify as the New Israel or the new people of God requires allegiance to Christ instead of obedience to the *mitzvot* (commandments). Following only *mitzvot* and in the absence of Christ, Jews are the "old" people. And is it not so that what is "growing old is ready to vanish away?" [13]

Here is the critical and essential difference between the two traditions. I agree with Olan that there is no possibility of dialogue unless the position stated in the Book of Hebrews and elsewhere in the New Testament is totally eliminated. A self–respecting Jew can never enter into dialogue or seek to develop areas of mutuality if Christians perpetuate the notion that Christianity is the completion of Judaism. The dilemma is that it may be impossible to cast this idea aside, *because it is logical.* If Christians admit that their belief–system is not superior to Judaism, then why continue that system? What do we do about such terms as the *new Moses*, the *new covenant*, the *new Jerusalem*, the *new people*? Even when we try to use Romans 9 through 11, we must remember, as Pawlikowski has pointed out, that this section of the New Testament "concludes with a conversionist motif."[14]

These doctrines basic to Christianity would seem to lead us inexorably to the conclusion—tenuous and tentative, one hopes—that "the continuous existence of the Jew is [no] more than an anachronism." Certainly it is true historically, at least up to the era when the notion of a "Judeo–Christian tradition" was promoted, that "Jews have been treated by Christianity as objects for conversion, as a people whose raison d'etre had ceased and whose Covenant had been displaced and supplanted by Christianity's new one."[15]

If Christianity is the completion of an incomplete and obsolete Judaism, then certainly Bonhoeffer is justified in writing:

> The church of Christ has never lost sight of this thought that the "chosen people" who nailed the Redeemer of the world to the cross must bear the curse for its action through a long history of suffering....But the history and suffering of this people, loved and punished by God, stands under the final home-coming of the people of Israel to God. And this home-coming happens in the conversion of Israel to Christ.[16]

Are there sources of mutuality short of bringing the Jews "home" through conversion to Christ? Are there fundamental agreements between the two traditions that go beyond the notion that Christianity is a complete Judaism? Does integrity exist in the idea of a "Judeo–Christian tradition" without resorting to the theory of a Judeo–Christian conspiracy against threats to their demise or alleged irrelevance? At this point, and based on what I have presented thus far, one certainly cannot argue easily for mutuality without sounding like a Brotherhood Week speaker at a Rotary luncheon.

Paul Tillich asked the critical question: "Are the common elements in both so strong that in comparison with other religions Judaism and Christianity belong to each other?"[17] In spite of everything said thus far, I answer Tillich's question affirmatively. The burden of affirmation rests on points of actual and potential agreement.

Sources of Mutuality

From my Jewish perspective, I find that Christians place considerable and, in my judgment, undue emphasis on the being of Jesus rather than on his teachings. As I read the Sermon on the Mount, I am moved profoundly by the convictions of this Jewish teacher. Although I may disagree with a few points in the sermon (dissent is intrinsically Jewish), I basically agree with the teachings of Jesus. They are Jewish exhortations based on a tradition with which Jesus felt completely at home. He felt no need for a "homecoming"; he was at home, just as I am at home with his ideas and values. Why do the Bonhoeffers of the world insist on the homecoming of Jews to Christ when we already are at home with Jesus and his message? To paraphase, by his fruits shall you know him. By the ideological fruits of Jesus, we can accept him; by his very being as something other than human–teacher–Jew–prophet, we refuse to know him. The source of compatibility here for both Jews and Christians is the potential enjoyment of the fruits. Can Christianity be complete with fruits, or must it by necessity enter into the ontological problems of Jesus as being?

Ontological issues are peripheral in Judaism. Discussions about the being of Yahveh or Moses or the prophets are rare, also irrelevant. The first commandment in Exodus 20 defines God in terms of the fruits of his being, the action he performs in bringing the Israelites out of bondage. The inital verse of the Hebrew Bible introduces God engaged in creating the universe. Yahveh–as–being is indefinable, and he is not subject to ontological scrutiny. But he is characterized predicatively, that is, by what he does. He creates and redeems. Without this twofold action, he is, as it were, not God.

Our mutuality would be in this possible conviction: *Jesus is as Jesus does.* I can accept Jesus predicatively, but not ontologically. Our source of agreement is in the teachings of Jesus. Jews and Christians can walk together to the mount and learn from the sermon.

Of course we must not lose sight of the obvious: Jesus was a Jew. He lived as a Jew and died as a Jew. I can identify with him as a Jew just as I can identify with his Jewish teachings. My acceptance of Jesus as a Jewish teacher is not necessarily the common position of my fellow Jews. To paraphrase Norman Cousins, Christians and Jews share a common perspective–neither will accept that Jesus was a Jew.

Moreover, I see in Jesus the personification of the *Malchut Shamayim*, the Kingdom of God, a utopian vision shared by Jews and Christians, when "Yahveh shall be king over all the earth; on that day Yahveh shall be one, and his name one."[18] Jesus personifies the fulfillment of the anticipated kingdom, the realization in his own deeds and personality of what could be for all humanity. His life was propadeutic; it pointed to the could–be and shall–be of human existence. The kingdom did not come in his lifetime, or thereafter, but he represented the possibility of the kingdom. I can accept this portrayal of the life of Jesus just as I can possibly accept it in the life of Isaiah, Hillel, Akiba, Gandhi, and King. Jesus inspires me to dream of and work for a future world where none will be afraid and rest will be given to the weary. His life and deeds point in the direction of an ideal society. Especially in moments of cynicism, he moves me forward to idealistic visions and hopes.

Jews and Christians share at least one other personality because of his fruits. Jewish tradition, primarily the midrashic literature, depicts Abraham as the first monotheist. He was called to bring the idea of one God to the world. He represents the emergence of monotheism from paganism, the human struggle from wandering Arameans to a holy people. He left his home to help others emerge. As the Midrash expresses it, "Why did Abraham have to go forth to the world? At home he was like a flask of myrrh with a tight–fitting lid. Only when it is open can the fragrance be scattered to the winds."[19]

Abraham also has a special place in the theology of the New Testament as a hero of faith: "By faith Abraham obeyed when he was called to go out to a place which he was to receive as an inheritance; and he went out, not knowing where he was to go. By faith he sojourned in the land of promise, as in a foreign land, living in tents with Isaac and Jacob, heirs with him of the same promise. For he looked forward to the city which has foundations, whose builder and maker is God."[20] In Judaism, Abraham is the father of a people and a faith. In Christianity, he is called "our father Abraham." We share Abraham and the Abrahamic vision of one God.[21]

But do we in reality share the concept of monotheism? Jews think of trinitarianism and incarnation as obstacles on the path of mutuality. Corporeal manifestations of God, however subtle, are completely execrable to Jews. Every composition throughout Jewish history that deals with the theology of Judaism to any degree underscores the idea that God is invisible and indivisible. That a triadic God transformed himself into human flesh and is consumable in the sacrament of Communion are sources of irreconcilable difference.

And yet, having said this, I take another leap of faith by suggesting that the Jewish and Christian concepts of God can be compatible when both traditions look at the various accounts of God in both "testaments" as figurative, as accounts of corporeal and sensuous imagery that point to the absolutely spiritual and unqualifiably abstract idea of God. God's stroll in Eden, his peregrinations about Sinai, his displeasure with Cain's inferior sacrifice can be placed in the same context of metaphor as tritheism and incarnation. Corporeal accounts and manifestations all point to the ultimate, infinite, unfathomable reality. But human beings imagine (create images of) God in human terms.

Tillich wrote that "a theology for which the trinitarian doctrine is something else than a symbolic description of the living God, who is one God, cannot claim to be Christian."[22] Even Jews, being human, are prone to conceive of God in corporeal terms.

> There is an interesting discussion of this issue between Maimonides and the Rabad (Rabbi Abraham ben David) in the Middle Ages. Maimonides, who was very deeply influenced by the truth system of Aristotle, said: He who believes that God is corporeal is considered a heretic. The Rabad, a very brilliant Kabbalist, said to Maimonides, in a little glossary note in the *Mishneh Torah*, that there were many Jews...who believed that God was corporeal. Even though belief in God's corporeality was a conceptual mistake, he was

not going to measure a person's being an idolator on the basis of his concepts! So there is a tradition within Judaism that was prepared to accept conceptual mistakes as long as this did not lead to experiential mistakes.[23]

By their fruits shall you know them! Are the results of believing in one God, of being monotheists, basically the same? If they are, Jews and Christians share a monotheistic faith.

Corporeality aside, both faiths share the idea of God as creator. Both believe the first verse of the Bible to be a primary principle of their traditions. God is the creative power of the cosmos, of all reality, generating order, harmony, and unity. We share the idea that the universe is dependable and predictable, based on the rational creativity of the "living God."

Furthermore, we share the conviction that this creator God makes moral demands. God is the source and ground of ethics. What is good is what the Lord requires. God demands justice, love, and humility. This ethical triad from the prophet Micah is a summation of the Sermon on the Mount. "Your will be done" is the essence of both Jewish and Christian ethics. It is expressed in *Pirke Avot* 2:41 as "Make his will as your will so that he may make your will as his will." Obedience to God is the springboard of Jewish and Christian ethics; every moral mandate flows from this.

What are the contents of the divine will? Jewish perception of God's will is universal in spirit and in substance. It is based on what is known as the heptalogue—the seven Noachitic Laws. According to Halachah, there are two kinds of non-Jews, idolators (*ovdim*) and Noachites (*b'nay Noach*). The Noachite is any non-Jew who assumes responsibility for carrying out the seven basic injunctions originally carried out by Noah (a non-Jew). The laws are the following: (1) Do not worship idols; (2) do not blaspheme the name of God; (3) do not kill; (4) do not engage in incest; (5) do not steal; (6) do not eat the flesh cut from a living animal; and (7) establish courts of justice. Maimonides states the normative position in Jewish law regarding these precepts: "Whoever professes to obey the seven Noachitic laws and strives to keep them is classed with the devout among the Gentiles and has a share in the world to come."[24] The last phrase is the rabbinic way of expressing the assurance of salvation.

Since the Christian is a Noachitic Gentile, according to Judaism, he is assured of salvation and enjoys equal ranking with the Jew. Maimonides, in fact, goes further in determining the position of Christians according to Halachah: "The Christians believe and confess, as do we, that the Bible is of divine origin and was revealed to our teacher Moses; only in interpretation of Scripture do they differ."[25] Again, we read in a letter by Maimonides, "In regard to your question concerning the Gentiles, you should know that God demands the heart, that matters are to be judged according to the intent of the heart. There is, therefore, no doubt that everyone from among the Gentiles who brings his soul to perfection through virtues and wisdom in their knowledge of God has a share in eternal blessedness."[26] One does not have to be Jewish to eat Levy's rye bread or to be saved.

In fact, according to the Talmud, "Anyone who denies idolatry is called a Jew."[27] The struggle against idolatry is possibly the focal issue of biblical Judaism, which even extends into talmudic Judaism as we learn from this statement: "Whoever denies idolatry is as if he fulfilled the entire Torah."[28] As Noachites, Christians share with Jews this important rejection of idolatry.

What is idolatry? Why was it considered to be such a nefarious and pernicious practice? We get some indication in the satirical description of the idolator in Isaiah 44. Deuteronomy equates both crime and punishment with regard to idolatry. The crime of idolatry (Deuteronomy 4:15–16) leads to the punishment of continued idolatry (4:28). Idolatry itself is a punishment according to biblical Judaism. The reason for this is based on the nature of idolatry. God is the supreme value of human existence, primarily because he is the one who demands justice, love, and humility. Ethical monotheism is the supreme value, and human beings are created to live ideally in the image of this ultimate value. To worship anything less than the righteous God is to live as something less than human. To be idolatrous is to debase the human–divine image itself. According to Fromm, human beings can be idolators in many ways other than the worship of wood or stone. We can worship words, machines, leaders, the state, power, political groups, science, neighbors' opinions, sexual powers, artifacts, nature, institutions, and so on. By identifying himself with a partial aspect of himself, man limits himself to this aspect; he loses his totality as a human being and ceases to grow. He is dependent on the idol, since only in submission to the idol does he find the shadow, although not the substance, of himself.[29] With this statement, we can understand why the punishment for idolatry is the same as the crime of idolatry in Deuteronomy. The crime of self–dehumanization is its own punishment.

As Noachites, Christians can share the Jewish protest against idolatry in all its manifestations. Jews and Christians can genuinely and with the utmost honesty work together to glorify the one God in their iconoclastic endeavors.

Maimonides, once again, recognized the mutuality of this struggle as we emerge together, like Abraham, from paganism to ethical monotheism. But he went even further in his vision of Jewish–Christian mutuality, envisioning messianic redemption coming not only from Jewish ideals, but from Christian and Islamic ideals as well. Both these religions can work with Judaism to prepare the way for the coming of the Messiah.[30] All three faiths possess a valid vision of the messianic era, and all three have the power to bring it about. This messianic faith, shared by Noachites, indicates something quite straightforward—the future can and must be better than the present. The prophetic refrain, "it shall come to pass in the end of days," implies not only the possibility of a world in which injustice, war, idolatry, slavery, and greed are eliminated, but that the world in which we presently live is unredeemed. The "end of days," the fulfilled kingdom of God, is still to come.

Thus we share the suffering of moral contradictions in a world yet to be redeemed. The Christian equivalent, in my judgment, is the concept of *parousia*, which is still awaited. The neglected idea of *parousia* came out of the first-century disappointments of Jews who believed in Jesus as Messiah. His life and crucifixion did not bring what the Messiah, in Jewish theology, was expected to achieve. Matthew's responding idea of *parousia* tells us that Christ will come again, that the kingdom of God through Christ will be realized in the future with his return.[31] This concept is a key factor in New Testament eschatology.

Both the notion of *y'mot ha-mashiach* (Messianic era) in Judaism and *parousia* in Christianity point to the teleological view of history both religions hold in common. History is the process of purposeful movement, not merely a random concatenation of events. The historic process is moving towards the ultimate goal, "in the end of days," of salvation and redemption. God operates in history as we have already noted with the first commandment of the decalogue. History is linked to divine judgment and, in the end, to divine fulfillment. Both *y'mot ha-mashiach* and *parousia* emerge not only from disappointments, but also from the vision of reality portrayed in the first chapter of Genesis. God creates the world, and it is good. But the goodness of God's creation is contradicted by the pervasive evidence of inhumanity throughout the world.

We come together, as Jews and Christians, not only in our shared suffering, not only in our shared hopes for a world redeemed, but also in our sense of vocation. We feel it is our sacred obligation to bring others either to Christ or to Torah as means to an end—the ultimate goal of knowing God and making his will our will. We share the audibility of God's voice exhorting us to merit the *y'mot ha-mashiach* or the *parousia*. We must come either to Christ or to Torah, respectively, if the days of good will and peace on earth are to be ushered in. Acceptance of this vocation must precede the "advent" or the "return" or the "era."

Suffering, vocation, protest, expectation, redemption—the long, arduous struggle of emerging from paganism to monotheism, from servitude to freedom, from bestiality to humanity is one of the most profound sources of our mutuality. How unfortunate that we allow the trees to obscure this majestic forest.

While it is much less obvious, I believe that we both can share in the continuing rebirth of Israel—the land and locus of Jesus' life and promise. Christianity was born in Israel, although the Jewish–Christians, headed by Peter and James, were not aware that they were engaged in the process of creating a new religion. They thought of themselves as Jews who had discovered the true Messiah. They were Jewish–Christians, not hellenized Christians. Their "Christianity" was planted in the soil of Israel; it grew out of the *mitzvot* of Palestinian Judaism. But this fruitful source of Christianity waned and died with the destruction of Jerusalem in 70 A.D.

A parallel therefore exists in the decline of both Palestinian Judaism and Palestinian Christianity. With the destruction of Jerusalem, Judaism moved to Babylonia for its continued growth, while Christianity moved to the hellenistic world for its continuance. In the latter part of the first century, when catastrophe was commonplace, another misfortune involved the eastward movement of Judeo–Christianity. This brought about the final and irrevocable schism, and from that moment, Jews of Israel and Babylonia could no longer accept the hellenized version of Judeo–Christianity nurtured by Paul as he journeyed to the cities of the Greco–Roman world. The demise of Israel as a national entity was a primary source of this fragmentation.

If the death of Israel parallels this disjunction, what does the birth, or rebirth, of Israel imply? Perhaps nothing. But I see a valid possibility that Israel's rebirth can be momentous not only for Jews but for Christians as a source of mutuality. Can it possibly signify the rebirth of Judeo–Christianity as it was originally lived and expressed by Peter, James, and their followers? Is it feasible and productive for a Christianity of the future to minimize the ideas of Paul and build on the ideas of Peter and James? Can the development of Israel and the flourishing of Israeli centers of Christian devotion become a catalyst for a return to pristine Christianity associated with the land loved by Jesus and the Twelve who followed him to Jerusalem? I believe the possibility is worth exploring as a rich and fruitful source of mutuality.

Similarly, another source of commonality could be one that may appear paradoxical when we consider the venomous remarks related to it in the New Testament. As strange as it may seem, I believe that Pharisaism is an ideological movement that we can share. While it is still a matter of grievous misunderstanding and friction between Jews and Christians, Pharisaism could bring us closer together instead of tear us apart. John Pawlikowski has enumerated the major innovations of the Pharisees, which happen to be shared by Christians.[32]

The Pharisees were responsible for the dramatic shift from temple to synagogue as the "central religious institution in Jewish life." The Christian idea of the church stems directly from the innovative growth of the synagogue in place of the temple and its sacrifical cult. The Pharisees also were responsible for the transformation from priesthood to rabbinate. The rabbi, as opposed to the priesthood with its intermediary and sacerdotal claims, came to be a model for the Protestant ministry. Another transformation effected by the Pharisees involved the change from temple sacrifices to home or community celebrations. This dramatic change may have influenced the development of the Eucharist as observance of the home supper shared by Jesus and the Twelve. In addition, the Pharisees were noted particularly for the growth of the Oral Torah, a legislative system for validating the continued and continuous interpretation of biblical statutes. This method allowed for the creative and flexible adaptation of Judaism to new conditions. So Christianity has experienced unending growth and adaptability through creative interpretations of canon law and theology. Consider also that the concept of resurrection in Christianity came naturally from the Pharisees, who introduced it as a central belief of rabbinic Judaism. In fact, it was a major point of disagreement between the Pharisees and the priestly Sadducees. Early Christianity and Pharisaism agree in their emphasis on this idea. Finally, Pharisaic ethics and the Sermon on the Mount are amazingly similar. To discover how true this is, read the brief tractate from the Talmud, *Pirke Avot*, referred to previously.

Since abusive language was heaped upon the Pharisees in the New Testament, it does appear strange to claim Pharisaic thought as a source of mutuality. But Pawlikowski indicates clearly why it is an authentic source. The abusive words are understandable when we realize that the Pharisees were vilifying each other. There were many kinds of Pharisees just as there are many kinds of Jews and Protestants. As Democrats and Republicans revile each other even though they are all Americans, so did the various kinds of Pharisees who, probably including Jesus and the Twelve, were all Jews. This fact did not prevent one Pharisaic party from calling another hypocrites.

Centrality of the Covenant

Whatever their contentions were, Jesus and his fellow Pharisees did not argue over the significance of the covenant in Jewish life. Here we return, once again, to a source of persistent friction between Jews and Christians, even though the situation could be the very opposite. Let me explain a possible way of bringing about a reversal of traditional enmity. As noted before, the enmity is based on the idea expressed in the Book of Hebrews that the "new" covenant is superior to the "old," that the new is necessary because the old is deficient. If the heart of Judaism is the covenant (the "old" one) then Judaism must also be deficient. After all, it has a bad heart. If the covenant of the new religion is better, then the new religion itself must be better. The logic here is impeccable, based as it is on the alleged inadequacy of the Jewish covenant. If we cannot find a resolution to this problem, this paramount point of contention, this foundation of Jewish–Christian relations (negative or positive), then the whole edifice of dialogue and mutuality crumbles. If there is no way out of the incomplete Judaism/complete Christianity imbroglio, then we must retreat to Olan's position that no dialogue is possible. But I believe in a way out, beyond the deletion of the Book of Hebrews from the New Testament.

Various writers concur that the convenant concept is central in Judaism. Eckardt writes that:

in recent biblical scholarship the Covenant has been stressed as a central—even, for some, the central—scriptural idea. Here is found a key to the existence of the Jewish people, to the meaning of its history, in the face of denigration as well as in the presence of blessings.[34]

Paul Ramsey goes even further in stressing the centrality of the covenant, saying, "Never imagine that you have rightly grasped a biblical idea until you have reduced it to a corollary of the idea of 'covenant.'"[35] Eckardt and Ramsey refer to the covenant in the singular. But there were several covenants in the Hebrew Bible alone. A covenant with Adam is implied in Genesis 1:1–25. The covenant with Noah was made explicit in Genesis 6 through 9. Then there is the covenant of Exodus, made with the Israelites at Sinai and sometimes referred to as the Sinaitic Covenant. The first two obligate mankind to obey the fundamental and universal principles of morality.

Several covenants, as specific phenomena occurring in time, seem to indicate the supremely important idea of covenanthood, or the state of moral obligation, the condition and experience of being covenanted. Of central importance in biblical thinking is the idea of the covenant, as Plato might have expressed it. There are many ways of *feeling covenanted*.

The individual covenants of the Hebrew Bible are important in their own ways. They may succeed each other, but no covenant supersedes a prior one. Each bears its own message. The implicit covenant with Adam conveys the idea of God's authority over all humanity. The Noachitic covenant was made with all living things with the renewal of the world after the Flood. These two covenants were universal; Adam and Noah were not Jewish. They covenanted all mankind regardless of religious convictions and practices. The condition of these covenants was the universal moral law. The Abrahamic covenant was missionary in the sense that it obligated Abraham to disseminate monotheism and to create a monotheistic people with the divine intention of teaching all peoples to accept the idea and will of the one God. The Sinaitic covenant transformed a horde of slaves into a missionary people who became obliged not only to teach monotheism by precept but also by example; hence, they were given many *mitzvot* to live by in order to discipline themselves into being a "kingdom of priests and a holy people."[36]

The covenant was used as an instrument of God for bringing about redemption, a state of existence that could come only through the acceptance of one God and his will. A new covenant was made in addition to those already mentioned—the covenant referred to in Ephesians and in Hebrews, a new mode of redemption, a new way of creating a beneficent relationship with God. It is the way of Christ. "But now in Christ Jesus you who once were far off have been broght near in the blood of Christ."[37] Thus we add the Christological covenant to the others. Have we reached the point, as Hebrews would possibly argue, where we experience a breach in the covenantal process of succeeding but not superseding stages, for centuries the religious experience of the Jewish community? If we eliminate the theology of the Book of Hebrews, we can understand the Christological covenant (as well as the Adamic, Noachitic, Abrahamic, and Sinaitic) as another stage in the spiritual aspiration of man to develop an optimal relationship with God. No covenant invalidates preceding or succeeding ones. Each in its own way creates a sense of being covenanted with ultimate reality. The "new" covenant is unique in its paramount purpose of extending monotheism to pagans and heathens. It it unique, but it is another covenant and not a supplanting covenant. It is superior, but all the covenants are superior in terms of their unique qualities and objectives.

The crucial problem, as already mentioned, is that many Christians consider the Christological covenant to be the final, perfect, and complete covenant, interpreting Ezekiel 16:60 to mean that this one is the "everlasting covenant" prophesied by Ezekiel. Predicted by the prophet, it is confirmed in Hebrews and Ephesians. If so, is there not a contradiction in Romans? There we read that to the Jews "belong the sonship, the glory, the *covenants*, the giving of the law, the worship, and the promises," keeping in mind also that "the gifts and the call of God are irrevocable" (emphasis added).[38]

In one passage of the New Testament, the "new" covenant is superior and supersedes the "old" covenant. In another passage, in the same New Testament, the covenants that belong to the Jews are "irrevocable." In one passage they are revoked; in another they are irrevocable. The Hebrew Bible has a number of contradictions also.

But the greatest problem of all is manifest not in scriptural contradictions, but in my own practice of quoting chapter and verse in the attempt to demonstrate either continuity or discontinuity, similarity or conflict. Why should I engage in the exercise of quoting minutiae from each Scripture? Am I so bound to details of chapter and verse that this is going to make a difference in my thinking about the theological issues of Judaism and Christianity? Why do I go to this trouble with details unless I am assuming the position of a fundamentalist or a literalist?

I speak primarily about the theophanies of Sinai and Calvary. Are they interpreted factually or figuratively? If we perceive each covenant as metaphorical—that is, symbolic of the content and quality of the divine–human relationship—then we should be able to accept the position enunciated by Jakob Petuchowski:

> Who am I to dictate to the Almighty into what covenantal relationships he can or cannot enter? Who am I to deny the salvation which the Christian believes to find in the Christ? And who is the Christian to call into question the redemptive function which I ascribe to the law? That my way may not be his way, nor his way mine, is a fact of life. It may be a regrettable fact. Or it may be a pleasant fact. For me it is, at any rate, an *interesting* fact. It makes religious life so much more fascinating and exciting. And if, as we do, we expect God to bear with us in all our diversity, we can certainly learn to imitate the ways of God by not only living with, but by actually appreciating the kind of religious pluralism which has become a fact of our lives.[39]

Who am I? Shall we say that the chapter–and–verse description of the covenantal experience is absolutely factual in that it happened precisely the way it is presented in the text? We are dealing with descriptions of divine revelation, human perceptions of the divine encounter. Who am I in terms of my personal perception of the divine? Are my perceptions perfect and infallible? Whatever we read in the Bible deals with divine truth as understood and perceived by finite man. What ultimate assurance do I have that my claims to understanding the infinite God are correct? Whether it is the experience of Noah, Abraham, Moses, Ezekiel, Jesus, or Paul, is it not possible (I would say necessary and unavoidable) for us to attribute a note of tentativeness and uncertainty to any experience of being covenanted? Whenever we seek—biblical man or modern man—to covenant with God and understand his will, are we not looking through a glass darkly? The introduction of fallible human perception into the covenant phenomenon is hinted at even in the Midrash, which says, "When God himself spoke only once at Mount Sinai, every individual apprehended the divine voice according to his own capacity."[40]

The covenant concept is a source of conflict between Judaism and Christianity only if we adopt a literalist position. If we think of the covenant as metaphor, then each covenant experience—a fallible, human perception of divine reality—becomes a symbol of the encounter between God and man and what the encounter signifies. Metaphorically, Jesus is the focus of the covenantal experience for Christians, just as the Torah is for the Jews. But of greatest importance is the convenantal experience itself. Schillebeeckx comes close to this idea in the very title of his book, *Christ: The Sacrament of the Encounter with God*. Both Sinai and Calvary are human experiences of the encounters with God. The experience itself—not its cosmic verity—is of greatest importance.

Does metaphorical thinking, however, diminish the sacral importance of the covenants for Christians and for Jews? I believe just the opposite. The metaphorical approach increases the significance. The specific covenant is a poetic image of an abstract concept. The image has persisted through the centuries primarily due to the power of imagery (Sinai) and the impact of personification (Jesus).

Metaphor is "an interpretation of reality...not through the medium of thought but through that of sensuous forms."[41] Fromm agrees with Cassirer that the metaphor or symbol is an idea transformed into a "sensory experience."[42] Aspects of ultimate reality vary all the time and cannot be contained in a single formula. Hence we need more than one covenant as metaphor to experience the abstract idea of covenanthood. This accounts for Eden, Ararat, Ur, Sinai, and Calvary. To make symbols of abstract ideas is innately and uniquely human. "Instead of defining man as *animal rationale*, we should define him as an *animal symbolicum*."[43] Langer concurs, stating:

> It is not the essential act of thought that is symbolization, but an act essential to thought, and prior to it. Symbolization is the essential act of mind; and mind takes in more than what is commonly called thought.... The brain is following its own law; it is actively translating experiences into symbols, in fulfillment of a basic need to do so.[44]

Abstract thoughts and concepts are recognized as well as shared because metaphor gives them sensory configurations we can easily accept due to our innate processes of symbolization. Thus the configuration may be an idyllic garden or a rainbow or a mountain in the wilderness or a cross. A conviction is not less true because it is expressed in metaphor and symbolism. On the contrary, it conveys more richly than any other medium possibly could—because it is the basic form of human cognition—the abstract ideas we cherish. The metaphor of Sinai, Calvary, and the other configurations of the covenant points to an ideation that is and has been true for centuries. Covenant is the metaphor for the divine–human encounter that evinces, in both the Jewish and the Christian experiences, a sense of moral obligation. The encounter is an affirmative and prescriptive answer—in every covenant—to the question, "Am I my brother's keeper?"

Covenant as idea indicates (1) God exists, (2) God is the creative power behind and beyond all existence, (3) God is the source of life, mandating his creatures to respect and revere life. This is the divine will expressed in every covenant: Come to the living God, and through him you will come to acknowledge the unconditional sanctity of life.

Founded on reverence for life and the ultimate worth of every person, both traditions are concerned profoundly with the theological-ethical implications and the social consequences of contemporary research in the genetic sciences. The following statement could have been written by either a Jew or a Christian: "Science is not the highest value to which all the others must be subordinated. Higher is the right of individuals to their physical and spiritual life and to their psychic and functional integrity."[45]

The Scriptures are called the "old" covenant and the "new" covenant, but not in the sense of the replacement of the old by the new. The old and new can be accepted as relative and chronological, not as theologically hierarchical, only if covenant is understood as metaphor leading to the greater truth that somehow God and man can meet, and in that meeting man can hear the answer to Cain's question—the first question asked of God.

If we can release ourselves from the straightjacket of literalism, we will have much more to share as Jews and Christians with the intrinsically human power and perception of metaphor to generate new, creative sources of commonality. Energies wasted on polemics will be channeled towards the ultimate values to which the metaphor is supposed to direct us. Acknowledging this function of the theological metaphor may lead to the acceptance of Lessing's epigram, "That which makes me a Christian in your eyes makes you a Jew in mine."[46]

The Final Answer

In the twelfth century, Don Pedro, king of Aragon, was confused about Judaism and Christianity. The king, of course, was a Christian. Having heard of a wise Jew in his land whose name was Ephraim Sancho, he asked that Ephraim be brought to him.

When Ephraim arrived before Don Pedro's throne, the king asked him, "Which faith is superior, yours or mine?"

When Ephraim heard the king's question, he was thrown into confusion. He said, "Our faith, O King, suits us better, for when we were slaves in Egypt, our God, by means of many wondrous miracles, led us out of bondage into freedom. For you Christians, however, your own faith is the better because by it you have been able to establish your rule over most of the earth."

When Don Pedro heard this, he was angered and said, "I didn't ask you what benefits each religion brings to its believers. What I want to know is, which is superior—yours or mine?"

Again Ephraim was troubled. He thought to himself, "If I tell the king that his religion is superior to mine, I will have denied the God of my fathers, and I'll truly deserve all the punishments of eternity. On the other hand, should I tell him that my religion is better than his, he will be sure to burn me at the stake."

To the king, Ephraim said, "If it please the king, let me ponder his majesty's question for three days, because it requires much reflection. At the end of the third day, I will come with my answer."

King Pedro said, "Let it be as you say."

For the three days that followed, the spirit of Ephraim was torn within him. He neither ate nor slept but put on sackcloth and ashes and prayed for divine guidance. But when the time arrived for him to see the king, he put all fear aside and went to the palace with his answer. When he came before the king, he looked downcast.

"Why are you so sad?" the king asked him.

Ephraim replied, "I am sad with good reason, because without any cause whatsoever I was humiliated today. Please be my judge in this matter, O King."

"Speak!" said Don Pedro.

Ephraim Sancho then began, "A month ago to this day a neighbor of mine, a jeweler, went on a distant journey. Before he departed, in order to preserve the peace between his two sons while he was away, he gave each of them a gift of a costly gem. Only today the two brothers came to me and said, 'Ephraim, give us the values of these gems and judge which is the superior of the two.'

"I replied, 'Your father himself is a great artist and an expert on precious stones. Why don't you ask him? Surely he will give you a better judgment than I.'

"When they heard this, they became enraged. They abused me. O King, judge whether or not my grievance is just."

The king shouted, "Those rogues have mistreated you without cause! They deserve to be punished for this outrage."

When Ephraim Sancho heard the king speak in this way, he rejoiced. "O King," he said, "your words are true and just. Each brother received a priceless gem. You have asked me, O King, which of the two gems is superior. How can I give you a proper answer? Send a messenger to the only expert of these gems—the one God of the Universe. Let him tell you which is the better."[47]

Notes

1. A. Roy Eckardt, *Elder and Younger Brothers* (New York: Schocken Books, 1973), p. 103.

2. David Noel Freedman, "An Essay on Jewish Christianity," *Journal of Ecumenical Studies* 6, no. 1 (Winter 1969): 81.

3. Levi A. Olan, "Christian–Jewish Dialogue: A Dissenting Opinion," *Religion in Life* 41, no. 2 (1972): 167.

4. Ibid., p. 169.

5. Bernard Heller, "About the Judeo–Christian Tradition," *Judaism* 1, no. 3 (July 1952): 260.

6. Arthur A. Cohen, "The Myth of the Judeo–Christian Tradition," *Commentary*, November 1969, p. 74.

7. Robert Gordis, "The Judeo–Christian Tradition: Illusion or Reality," *Jewish Frontier*, April 1965, p. 17.

8. Cohen, "Judeo–Christian Tradition," p. 77.

9. Ibid., p. 77.

10. Hebrews 9:15.

11. Robert Aron, "Judaism and Christianity," *Encounter Today* 7, no. 3–4 (Summer–Autumn 1972): 100–101.

12. W.D. Davies, "Christianity and Judaism: A Christian View," *Jewish Heritage*, Winter 1962, p. 8.

13. Hebrews 8:13.

14. John T. Pawlikowski, "The Jewish/Christian Diagloue: Assessment and Future Agenda," *Conservative Judaism* 32, no. 2 (Winter 1979): 42.

15. Balfour Brickner, "The Covenant between Us," *Concern* May–June 1969, p. 16.

16. Bonhoeffer, quoted in Olan, "Christian–Jewish Dialogue," pp. 160–161.

17. Paul Tillich, "Is There a Judeo–Christian Tradition?" *Judaism* 1, no. 2 (April 1952): 106.

18. Zechariah 14:1.

19. Genesis Rabbah 39:2.

20. Hebrews 11:8–10.

21. Romans 4.12.

22. Paul Tillich, "Is There a Judeo–Christian Tradition?" *Judaism* 1, no. 2 (April 1952): 107.

23. David Hartman, "Jews and Christians in the World of Tomorrow," *Immanuel*, Spring 1976, pp. 80–81.

24. Maimonides, Mishneh Torah, Melachim 10:2.

25. Pe'er ha–Dor 50.

26. Maimonides, letter to Chasdai ha–Levi.

27. Talmud Bavli Megillah 13a.

28. Sifray III to Numbers 15:22.

29. Erich Fromm, *You Shall Be as Gods* (New York: Holt, Rinehart and Winston), p. 44.

30. Mishneh Torah, Melachim 10:14.

31. Matthew 24:3, 27, 39.

32. Pawlikowski, "The Jewish/Christian Dialogue," pp. 43–46.

33. Ibid.

34. Eckardt, *Brothers*, p. 36.

35. Paul Ramsey, quoted in Will Herberg, "Judaism and Christianity: Their Unity Difference," *The Journal of Bible and Religion* 21, no. 2 (April 1935): 69.

36. Exodus 19:6.

37. Ephesians 2:13.

38. Romans 9:4; 11:29.

39. Jakob Petuchowski, "Jewish/Christian Dialogue: The Religious Basis for Pluralism," *Origins* 6, no. 47 (May 12, 1977): 746.

40. Exodus Rabbah 5:9.

41. Ernst Cassirer, *An Essay on Man* (New York: Doubleday/Anchor Books, 1944), p. 188.

42. Erich Fromm, *The Forgotten Language* (New York: Grove Press, 1951), p. 12.

43. Cassirer, *Essay on Man,* p. 44.

44. Susanne K. Langer, *Philosophy in a New Key* (Cambridge: Harvard University Press, 1973), pp. 41–42.

45. Pope John Paul II, quoted in *The New York Times*, July 5, 1981, p. 12.

46. Gotthold E. Lessing, *Nathan the Wise,* 4.7.

47. Nathan Ausubel, *A Treasurey of Jewish Folklore* (New York: Crown Publishers, 1948), pp. 43–44.

Index

Persistent Prejudice: Perspectives on Anti-Semitism

Prepared by Joan Kalyan

Abraham, 137–38
Adams, Hannah, 88
Adams, Henry, 93
Adams, John, 87–88
Age, determiner of anti-Semitism, 67, 72
Aliya, 115, 121
Alkalai, Yehudah, 129, n.4
The Ambassadors, Henry James, 94
American College Dictionary, 83
American immigration quotas, 76; public opinion concerning, 77
American Jewish Congress, 125
American literature: anti-Semitism in, 83–96; Yiddish dialect in, 90
Anschluss, 76
Anti-Jewish polemics, in ancient world, 21
Anti-Judaism, 83
Anti-refugee movement, in America, 76–77
Anti-Semitic myths, 3, 45, 85, 96
Anti-Semitism: in antiquity, 18–19; fourth century, 12, 16; fifth century, 12; High Middle Ages, 5, 20–22, 85; Elizabethan England, 101–102; Reformation, 23–24; Counter-Reformation, 25; eighteenth century, 5; nineteenth century, 5, 36, 111; twentieth century, 5, 36
Anti-Semitism: determiners of, 67–76, 72; index to health of society, 64; political tool, 25; racial, 21; in scholarship, 19–20; secular, 24
Anti-Semitism: roots of, 2–3, 5, 11, 15–19; in Christian theological teaching, 20–21
Anti-Semitism, scholarship about: by Americans, 60, 67–69; by

Europeans, 64; neglect by Americans, 60, 64
Anti-Semitism in America, 59, 69, 72; economic causes, 59, 68, 71–72; the New Right, 71–72
Anti-Semitism in America: nineteenth century, 67–68, 71–74; early twentieth century, 63, 74–75; during World War II, 76–77
Applebaum, Shimon, 19
Arab–Israel war, first, 124–25
Arab Jewish tensions, 115, 118, 121, 123–24
Archetypal images of Jews in literature, 84–85; Jewish daughter as exotic erotic, 89, 91
Arendt, Hannah, 47
Aron, Robert, 135
Arthur Mervyn, Charles Brockden Brown, 88

Back-to-Africa movement, 114, 118–19
Balfour, Arthur James, 115
Balfour Declarations, 115–16, 126
"Ballad of the Jew's Daughter," 85
"Banality of evil," 48
Barabas, 84, 101
Baron, Salo, 15
Baum, Gregory, 12, 16, 17
Bauer, Yehuda, 64
Begin, Menachem, 125
Bernadotte, Count Folke, 124–25
Bevin, Ernest, 126
Biblical traditions, exclusivity of, 39
Black anti-Semitism, 66–67, 72
Black nationalism, 118–20
Blood libel, 22, 84
Blyden, Edward Wilmot, 107, 109–113

Boas, Frank, 65
Bonacich, Edna, 72
Bonhoeffers, 136
Book of Hebrews, 18, 143, 145
Bouton, Archibald Lewis (Dean of New York University), 74
Brown, Charles Brockden, 88
Brown, Elmor (Chancellor of New York University), 74
Brown, Raymond, 17
Bunche, Ralph, 107, 124-26

Calley, William, 50-52, 57, n.36
Canterbury Tales, Geoffrey Chaucer, 84, 100-01
Caputo, Philip, 49-50
Century Club, 73
Chamberlain, Houston Stewart, 25
Chamberlain, Neville (Prime Minister), 122
Chaucer, Geoffrey, 101
"Christian theology of contempt," 12
Christian-Jewish relations, 19-20
Christians, salvation of, according to Judaism, 139
Chrysostum, John, 16
Civil War (United States), 109
Clarel, Herman Melille, 93
Clark, Ruth, 66, 71
Clothing, to mark Jews, 22
Cognative dissonance, 38
Cohen, Arthur, 134
Cohen, Jeremy, 21
Cohen, Naomi, 68
Columbia University, 74
Conversion of the Jews, 88
Corporality of God, 138
Coughlin, Father Charles, 76
Cousins, Norman, 137
Covenant, 135, 143-46
Crisis, 117
Crusade, First, 3
Crutchfield, Richard, 65

Daniel Deronda, George Eliot, 96
Davies, Alan T., 14-15
Davies, W.D., 135
Dawidowicz, Lucy, 67
Dearborn Independent, 65, 75
Deicide charge, 12, 13, 22
Deir Yacin Massacre, 124
Demonification of Jews, in literature, 84
Destruction of the Temple (70 B.C.E.), 69
Diamond, Sander, 71
Dibelius, Bishop Otto, 6, 38
Dinnerstein, Leonard, 69, 71

Dissonance reduction, 38
Dominicans, 5, 21-22
Drieser, Theodore, 95-96
Du Bois, W.E.B., 107, 116-17, 122, 125-27

Eckardt, Roy A., 133, 144
Education, determiner of anti-Semitism, 66-67, 71
Edward I, king of England, 100
Eichmann, Adolf, 47, 48; trial of, 60
Eliot, George, 96
Eliot, T.S., 95
Elizabeth I, 102
English literature, anti-Semitism in, 84-85
Epistle to the Hebrews, 18, 143, 145
Ethan Brand, Nathaniel Hawthorne, 92
Ethical monotheism, 140
Ethics, Jewish and Christian, 139
Ettinger, Shmuel, 64
Expulsion of Christians from the Synagogue, 15
Expulsion of Jews: England, 100; Saxony (1536), 36; Spain and Portugal (fifteenth century), 22
Ezekial, 145

Frackenheim, Emil, 59, 63
Fall of Jerusalem, meaning of, 17
Ferris, William H., 119
Fiedler, Leslie, 90, 95
Fielding, Achsa, 89
"Final solution," 4, 5, 45
Flannery, Edward, 15
Ford, Henry, 65, 75
Fourth Lateran Council, 22
Frank, Leo, 69
Franklin, John Hope, 118
Fransciscans, 5, 21-22
Fromm, Erich, 140

Gager, John G., 17-19
Garvey, Marcus, 107, 118-22
Genesis, 141, 144
Genocide, 31; cultural conditions for, 44-46; guilt-free, 44, 46-48, 52-53; political conditions, 44, 48-53; preconditions, 6-9, 49; psychological conditions, 44, 46-48, 52-53
Gentiles, salvation of, according to Judiasm, 139
Gerber, David, 72
"Gerontion," T.S. Eliot, 95
"Golden Mouth," 16
Gordis, Robert, 134

Gospel of John, 15, 18
Green, Robert, 101–102
Greer, Germaine, 99
Guiana, 122
Guilt-free massacre, 44, 46–48, 52–53

Halachah, 139
Halpern, Ben, 65
Handlin, Oscar, 68, 71
Harap, Louis, 87–90
Harvard University, 74
Hawthorne, Nathaniel, 91–92
Heller, Bernard, 134
Heptalogue, 139
Hertzberg, Arthur, 24
Herzl, Theodor, IU–12
Hess, Moses, 110
Hess, Rudolf, 47, 53, 55 n.19
Higham, John, 64–65, 68, 71, 73–74
Hilberg, Raul, 44
Himmler, Heinrich, 48
History, teleological view of, 141
Hitler, Adolf, 45, 99, 104, n.1, 120–21; dehumanization of Jews, 45; Reichstag speech (January 30, 1939), 40
Hofstadter, Richard, 71
Holocaust, 2, 11, 123; American apathy to, 60, 76; causes of, 21; meaning of, according to Lutheran theologians, 35
Homiliaeae adversars Judaeos, John Chrysostum, 16
Host desecration charges, 22
Howe, Irving, 94

Idolatry, 138, 140
Images of the Jew, 70–71
Incarnation, Jewish response to, 138
Indoctrination, rituals of, 49–50; Austrian police force, 50; Nazi SS, 50–51; U.S. Marine Corps, 50
Innitzer, Cardinal, 51
Irving, Henry, 100
Isaac, Jules, 12
Islamic ideals, 140

James, Henry, 93–94
Jefferson, Thomas, 87–88
Jerusalem, destruction of (A.D. 70), 142
Jesus, 143, 145–46
The Jew of Malta, Christopher Marlowe, 101

Jewish refugees, from Nazi Germany, 75–76
Jewish-Gentile relations, in the ancient world, 18
Jews, agents of Satan, 22–23, 61, 90; clothing to mark, 22; conversion of, 88; crimes attributed to, 2, 12–13, 22–23, 61, 75, 83–84, 90; disconfirming other, 38–39; legal victimization of, 3; Puritan attitude toward, 87–88
Jews, expulsions: from England, 100; Saxony (1536), 36; Spain and Portugal (fifteenth century), 22
Jews, images and stereotypes, 45, 70–71; in literature, 3, 61, 70–71; 89–92, 96
Jews, population in America: eighteenth century, 86; nineteenth century, 89
Judas, 85
Judensau, 22
Judeo-Christian relations, 133–36
Judeo-Christian tradition, 134–36

Kalischer, Rabbi Zvi Hirsch, 110
Kallen, Horace, 65
Katz, Jacob, 64
Kean, Edmund, 100
Kenya, 112
Kith and Kin oath, 51
Kristallnacht, 37, 76
Ku Klux Klan, 75

Language as cultural weapon, 45–46, 51
Larimer, George Horace, 76
Lassen, Christian, 83
Le Carre, John, 96
Liberia, UO, U9–20, 123
Lindbergh, Charles, 75
Lippard, George, 90
Lippmann, Walter, 65
Literature, images of Jews in, 61, 70–71, 84, 90, 92, 96
Loeb, Jacques, 73
Lopez, Aaron, 88
Lopez, Roderigo, 102
Lowell, A. Lawrence (President of Harvard), 74
Luther, Martin, 5–6, 23, 31–40, 45; advocating violence against the Jews, 36–37; demonization of Jews, 36, 39–40; doctrine of faith, 31–32; refutation of Jewish reading of Scriptures, 33–35
Lynch, Hollis, 110

Lynching of blacks in America, 114

Maimonides, Moses, 138–140
Marine Corps, United States, 50
Marlowe, Christopher, 84, 89, 99, 101
Marr, Wilhelm, 83
Martire, Gregory, 66, 71
Marx, Gary, 66, 72
Mass murder, preconditions for, 6–9, 49
Mather, Cotton, 88
McMahon-Hussein agreement (1915), 115
McWilliams, Carey, 67, 71
Medieval and modern anti-Semitism, links between, 23
Medieval Christianity, 20
Melville, Herman, 92–93
Mencken, H.L., 95–96
The Merchant of Venice, William Shakespeare, 61, 99–104
Merkl, Peter, 52
Messianic era, 141
Michael, Louis, 120
"Middleman minorities," 72–73
Midrash, 146
Midrashic literature, 137
Milgram, Stanley, 47, 52
Minim, curse against the, 15
The Monks of Monk's Hall, George Lippard, 90
Monotheism, 137–39, 144
Mosse, George, 70
Murphy, Gardiner, 65
Mutuality, between Christianity and Judaism, 134–42
My Lai, 50
Mystery Play cycles, 84

NAACP, 116, 123, 127
Nashe, Thomas, 85, 102
Nazi Germany, 4, 6; obedience to authority in, 47, 50–51; rise of, 76; image of Jews in, 45, 70
New Right, 71–72
New Testament, 12–13, 14, 18
Noachites, 139–40
Noachitic Laws, seven, 139

Oberman, Heiko, 23
Olan, Levi, 133–134
On the Jews and Their Lies, Martin Luther, 6, 7, 23, 32–34, 37–38
Oxford English Dictionary, 83

Palestine, 109–115, 117–24, 126–27; partition of, 121–24, 128

Palestine Commission, 124
Palestinian Christianity, decline of, 142
Palestinian Judaism, decline of, 142
Pan-Africa movement, 116–17
Park, Robert E., 65
Parousia, 141
Passion Plays, 22, 84
Patristic Period, 15–19
Pawlikowski, John, 25, 135, 142–43
Peel Commission, 121
Petuchowski, Jakob, 146
Pharisees, 142–43
Pilate, Pontius, 13
Pinsker, Leo, 112
Plague (fourteenth century), 22
Pograms, 4, 21; in Czarist Russia, 113, 115
Poliakov, Leon, 64
Political socialization, 48–49, 52, 55–56, n.24
Pope John Paul II, 11
Populist movement, 75
Porter, Katherine Anne, 94
Preconditions for mass murder, 6–9, 49
"Preservation," Christian tradition of, 20–21
The Prioress's Tale, Geoffrey Chaucer, 101
Protestant Reformation, 31
The Protocols of the Elders of Zion, 25, 36
Psychological archetypes, 84
Puritan identification with Jews, 65
"Purity of blood" laws, 25

Quaker City, George Lippard, 90
Quota systems, 74–75

Rabad (Rabbi Abraham ben David), 138
Rabbinate, 142
Race, determiner of anti-Semitism, 67, 72
Racial anti-Semitism, 21
Racial myths and stereotypes, 52, 54, n.6, 70, 75, 84–85
Rahv, Philip, 92, 94
Ramsey, Paul, 144
Reformation, 31
Refugees, from Nazi Germany, 76
"Reprobation," Christian tradition of, 21
Retailer-consumer antagonisms, 72
Reuther, Rosemary, 13–14, 16, 17–18, 20

Rhetoric, as cultural weapon, 45–46, 51
Ribuffo, Leo, 71
Ring Cycle, 99, 104, n.1
Robeson, Paul, 127
Roosevelt, Theodore, 113
Rose, Arnold, 69, 71
Rothschild, Lord, 115
Rubenstein, Richard, 72

Sandmel, Samuel, 13
Sarna, Jonathan, 65
Sartre, Jean–Paul, 70
Saturday Evening Post, 76–77, 90
Schneider, William, 71
Schuyr, George, 127–28
Second coming of Christ, 88
Secular anti–Semitism, 24
Seligman, Joseph, 73
Sereny, Gitta, 43
Sermon on the Mount, 136, 139, 143

Shakespeare, Wlliam, 61, 84, 99–100
Shemoneh Esreh, 15
Shylock, 84, 99–104
Simon, Marcel, 15
Six Day War, 128
Sobibor extermination camp, 47
Social discrimination, in America, 73
Social science literature on anti–Semitism, 65–67
St. Augustine, 21–22
St. Ignatius of Loyola, 25
St. Paul, 18
St. Teresa of Avila, 25
Stangl, Franz, 43, 47–48, 50–51
State of Israel, creation of, 123–24
State policies against the Jews: conversion, 3, 21; expulsion, 3, 21; annihilation, 3
Stern, Menahem, 19
Stewart, Barbara, 76
Stiles, Ezra (President of Yale), 88
Straus, Nathan, 73
Supercessionism, 12
Sykes–Picot agreement, 115
Synoptic gospels, 18

Talmud, burning of, 22
Talmudic study, used against Jews, 22 Theological differences between Jews and Christians, 108

Theological polimics of Patristic period, 21
Tilch, Paul, 136, 138
Torah, 143, 146
Toynbee, Arnold, 69
Treblinka extermination camp, 47
Trilling, Lionel, 85
Trinutarianism, Jewish response to, 138
Troeltsch, Ernst, 31–32
Truman, Harry, 126–27
Turner, Bishop Henry McNeal, 114
The Unfortunate Traveller, Thomas Nashe, 85, 102

United Nations, 123, 127
Universal Negro Improvement Association (UNIA), 118–19, 121
Universe of Moral Obligation, 7, 39

Vidal, Gore, 94
Vladimir Jabotinsky–Begin Revisionists, 126
Voltaire, 24–25
Von Gelt, Gabriel, 90

Wagner, Richard, 99, 104, n. 1
Wallimann, Isidor, 72
Wandering Jew, 92
Washington, Booker T., 107, 113–116
Weber, Max, 72
Welles, Max, 72
Welles, Orson, 99
Wharton, Edith, 95
Whitaker, Alexander, 46
"White Paper," 121–22
White, Walter, 123
Wiesel, Elie, 43, 69
Wilken, Robert L., 16–17
Wolfsheim, Meyer, 90

Yahveh, 137
Yerushalmi, Yosef Hayim, 20–21
Yinger, J. Milton, 1
Y'mot ha-mashiach (Messianic era), 141

Zionism, 85, 109–115, 117–18, 120–21, 123, 126; black sympathy for, 107–129; black anti-Zionism, 127–28
Zionist Congress, 111–12
zu Falkenau, Count Wolf Schlick, 33

Authors

Michael N. Dobkowski is associate professor of religious studies at Hobart and William Smith Colleges. He is the author of *The Tarnished Dream: The Basis of American Anti-Semitism* (1979) and several works on the Holocaust.

Eugene J. Fisher is executive secretary of the Secretariat for Catholic–Jewish Relations of the National Conference of Catholic Bishops in Washington, D.C. His most recent book is *Twenty Years of Catholic–Jewish Relations* (1986), coedited with James Rudin and Marc Tanenbaum.

Herbert Hirsch chairs the Department of Political Science at Virginia Commonwealth University.

Richard Kazarian, Jr., is on the faculty of the University of Rhode Island.

Carole Kessner teaches in the Department of Comparative Literature and Judaic Studies at the State University of New York at Stony Brook. She has produced and delivered lecture programs for the *Jewish People's University of the Air,* presented on National Public Radio.

Richard L. Rubenstein is Lawton Distinguished Professor of Religion at Florida State University.

Nicholas A. Sharp is on the Nontraditional Studies faculty at Virginia Commonwealth University.

Jack D. Spiro is Rabbi of Temple Beth Ahabah in Richmond, Virginia, and director of Judaic studies at Virginia Commonwealth University.

Robert Weisbord is a professor of history at the University of Rhode Island. His article included in this collection is based on his book *Israel in the Black American Perspective* (1985).